Sociology, Morals and Mystery

By the same author

The Life of John Maynard Keynes
Towards a Dynamic Economics
Reforming the World's Money
Money
Foundations of Inductive Logic

International Economics
(Cambridge University Press)

Sociology, Morals and Mystery

*The Chichele Lectures
Delivered in Oxford
under the auspices of
All Souls College,
1970*

ROY HARROD

Macmillan

St. Martin's Press

First published 1971 *by*
MACMILLAN AND CO LTD
London and Basingstoke
Associated companies in New York Toronto
Dublin Melbourne Johannesburg and Madras

Library of Congress catalog
card no. 71–143998

SBN 333 12341 7 (hard cover)

Printed in Great Britain by
R. & R. CLARK LTD
Edinburgh

Contents

Introduction

WHEN I had the honour of being invited to deliver the Chichele Lectures this year, my first choice of a suitable subject was the logic of induction; but I was informed that this was not within the rubric of allowed subjects. And so for a couple of months I had it in mind that I ought to deliver lectures on the subject on which, perhaps, I was best qualified, namely the international monetary system. I was a little depressed by this idea, as this is at present a well-worn theme. Also, there were technical difficulties. Many members of my audience were not likely to have read my recent book on *Money*, so that, in order to give an intelligible narrative, I should have to repeat some things that I had already set out in that book. It is true that there are always new things to say about international money, as the scene continues to change rapidly. An appropriate place for such additional matter would be in a revised edition of the book.

While I was pondering upon this problem, a complex idea suddenly came into my mind. I truly believe that it was within a split second that I thought of the general title of the course of lectures and also of the sub-titles of each separate lecture. In a certain sense one may even say that the course, apart from details, was composed in that second.

The purpose of this Introduction is to give some account

of the interconnection, as I conceive it, of the different subjects named, their relation to each other may not at first be
obvious.

My background thought was the great importance of
social study in this phase of our history – one might almost
say, supreme importance. It must not be inferred that I
regard sociology as a suitable subject for instruction at universities. In its present phase it is very amorphous, and for
university study one requires subjects that are sufficiently
mature for them to be good instruments in training the
thinking power of students.

Although fundamental physics is, I believe, at present
progressing rather slowly, we have rapid progress in many
branches of physical science, and even more rapid progress
in the technologies concerned with material objects. One
may even think that in the not too far distant future the
progress of technology may be so great as to enable man to
provide himself with all his more important physical needs.
This is, perhaps, subject to the population explosion not
presenting too severe a problem.

It is not so evident that we are making progress in our
understanding of social relations. Some even think that we
are slipping backward, not only relatively to the problems
confronting us, which are becoming more complex, but
absolutely. The problems are many and various. One group
of problems that has gained special attention recently is that
concerned with urban renewal in areas fairly near the
centres of American cities – the downgrading of certain
areas into slums, de-housing on a large scale, the lack of
a decent community spirit in neighbourhoods, and racial
tensions. At the other end of the world, one may think of
problems in some less developed countries, where the
organisation of life needed to implement material progress
may not be consistent with well-established tribal habits.
These old habits, which may look rather obsolete to those

already advanced in material progress, often embody patterns of emotion and conduct that serve important purposes. It is desirable to get an adaptation that preserves what is valuable in tribal institutions. A mere destruction of them may leave a dangerous vacuum. It is to be remembered that advanced societies embody many aspects of a 'way of life', perhaps not often noticed, because they are taken for granted, that have in fact been evolved over the course of many generations, even centuries.

Such problems, varied and widespread, present a great challenge. Are we facing it? I confess that I am somewhat uneasy. It was this background of uneasiness that was my main motive for endeavouring to deal with the subjects of these lectures.

As an economist, I am not at the centre of thinking about the kind of problems that I have just mentioned, although economics is, of course, highly relevant to them. While I shall display some scepticism in my lecture on the 'contribution of economics' – but I hope not so much as to give offence to my professional colleagues – I would suppose that economics is in a much more advanced and satisfactory condition than other branches of sociology. It is of these other branches that we are at present sorely in need.

Since I am an economist, my knowledge of what is on foot in these other branches is due to what, so to speak, I overhear being said at the next table. I do not like the sound of the language, which is all too often jargon, or the methods of approach to the problem that seem to be implied. I was much disturbed by the trash, embodied in student manifestos, or in reports of student committees, that came from time to time on to the desk of my office in the University of Pennsylvania. I am confident that similar nonsense is circulated in other universities also. 'Office' is the American for what we call our 'room', or 'rooms', in college here. 'Study' is an acceptable alternative name. 'Office' is bad in this connection, because it connotes a place for the despatch of business, which is not the way in which we ought to regard the room assigned one in a university for studying, teaching and, above all, thinking.

Realising that one certainly must not rely exclusively on what is overheard at the next table, I spent some weeks at the University of Pennsylvania in reading recent books on sociology, as recommended by experts, and by the books themselves. It may be interesting to note that my reading needs took me to five different libraries in the University. This may reflect the present condition of sociology and implies no criticism of the library organisation there. I hoped by this course of reading to assuage my uneasiness; but things turned out the other way round.

Part of my uneasiness relates to representations by students more serious than the foolish manifestos to which I have already referred. There is a desire that the subject-matter of courses should be more 'relevant' to current problems and to what the student may become involved in after he has completed his degree. The need for such relevance is obvious in the case of doctors and engineers. In Oxford many of us discouraged would-be lawyers from reading law when at the University. They could work later for their professional examinations. We thought that subjects like Greats (classics including philosophy), Modern Greats (philosophy, politics and economics) and even History – ancient history is to be preferred to modern in this regard – gave a better training for the brain, later to be subjected to the exacting process of relating the facts of a disputed case to legal precedents, than would any university course in law itself, however well devised.

This idea of 'relevance' is rather dangerous. In relation to the current problems of the day, the instructors would be hardly human if they did not have some prejudices; in fact we should think them a poor sort of people if they did not.

But the subject-matter of what they have to impart should be so devised as to ensure that prejudice will not intrude into the instruction. Training in how to be strictly objective is of the utmost importance, and this may be jeopardised if the course deals with matters on which the teacher has prejudices. It is much more important that the subject-matter should be of a mind-training character than that it should have any bearing on the student's subsequent avocation.

I recall that, when sitting in the Cosmos Club in Washington in 1930, to have a haircut, the barber, a famous character in Washington in those days, remarked to me, 'The trouble about this country is that there are too many half-arsed graduates around'. What would he think of the present situation?

To add to my uneasiness, I have the idea that many who go to universities here, and still more so in the United States, do so, not because they are passionately interested in culture or aspire to having a well-trained brain, but because they believe, probably rightly, that the degree tag will help them to get better-paid jobs. I remember that, when I was a young don at Christ Church, I was furious when I learned that some important British firm had brushed aside the university qualifications of a former pupil as being of no relevance. Now, after many years, I wonder if I was right. If the training has been good, the young man will find it easy to overhaul his competitors in climbing the ladder to higher pay in his firm. This might shift the emphasis in the student's mind from the degree tag on to making sure that his studies were really equipping him well for thinking, a process in which he has to co-operate.

A charming young lady said to me the other day that she did not feel that the instruction at a (new) university here, of which she was an undergraduate, took enough trouble to develop the 'creative' potentialities of the students. So, when one gets to a university, the instruction given should make one 'creative'. That is something different.

Of course, undergraduates can be, and often are, 'creative'. I would think that the most important area in which undergraduates display creativeness is in making good jokes. That is not derogatory. A sense of humour is surely one of the highest qualities of civilised man. But I am now doing less than justice to the very creative group of undergraduates with whom it was my good fortune to mingle at New College in 1919–22. They did make very good jokes, but their creativity covered a much wider field. It consisted in their style of speaking and in the nature of their comments on friends, college episodes, current events, books, plays, political characters and even characters of the past. I think of figures like Stephen Tomlin, Maurice Bowra, Idris Deane-Jones, Henry Andrews, Eric Strauss, Hugh Francis, Harry Scott-Stokes, Douglas Woodruff, and, in some sense dominating them all, J. B. S. Haldane. These were all highly creative. And there were others. Bull, whose Christian name I don't think any of us knew, was creative in his quiet way too. And their creativity was subject to the severe intellectual discipline of Cyril Radcliffe.

And I had the good luck a few years later, when I was a young don at Christ Church, to be in contact with a highly creative group of undergraduates, totally different from the New College set, indeed, worlds apart, whose leader was Harold Acton. I have tried to give a brief description of them in my contributions to the biography of Brian Howard.

It is absolutely clear to me that neither of these sets owed anything, as regards their creativeness, to tutors. In this respect they were far superior to the available tutors. I think that they learned from each other, by mutual stimulus. Each was supplied with an inspiration to give greater rein to his own creativeness by the appreciation of the others. That should have been my answer to the young lady. 'Do not hope to be instructed by tutors in creativeness. Develop for yourself what in you lies and find other students who are on the same track and will be appreciative'.

On the whole the New College dons were not creative, or capable of inspiring others in that direction. Looking back, I can only recall two who might be deemed creative, Johnnie Myres and Alec Smith. But their interests were on the whole apart from and different from ours. The task of the dons was to train their pupils in powers of thinking and expression and in methods of investigation. I believe that the New College dons did this very efficiently, and that their instruction was of much help to the bright young things of my time in their subsequent careers.

I have, after all, with the permission of the Warden of All Souls, devoted a half of one lecture to the logic of induction. This is perhaps the section that is furthest removed from my central theme. My idea was not that it is always needful to revert to logical substructure in considering a subject. On the contrary, I hold that there tends to be far too much about methodology in some sociological writing. My motive was a more subtle one. Cousin to my uneasiness about sociology has been a much deeper and more important uneasiness about the condition of the logic of induction. I have had this for the greater part of my life. I detect a certain defeatism in this area. There has been created, of course, the great structure of mathematical logic, which one associates especially with the names of Russell and Whitehead, who had, however, their predecessors as well as successors. This structure seems to be somewhat detached from the working logic of the sciences. It does not give a clue about how to argue from experience. It does not even seem to embody in its own structure clear evidence that it will be applicable to the universe in which we live. On the other side we have seen failure to establish how we can argue from experience.

Various more recent approaches have in common a philosophy that may loosely be called pragmatism. I reject all forms of pragmatism.

I have set forth my own views in my book on logic. My claim is that my method of establishing the validity of argument from experience, by dividing a continuum into a number of equal aliquot parts, a purely intellectual and rational process, would apply to any kind of universe whatever, however unlike the one that we know, provided only that it contained continua. If the world in which we lived contained no continuities, then we could never gain any knowledge at all about it by any methods available to us. Various specific methods of inductive argument flow from the axiom that we can trust experience, and they depend essentially upon it. The validation of induction restores muscle to our thinking and expels defeatism. Practitioners of the physical sciences do not need to bother much with these questions in most cases because their own specific methods of procedure have long been established; they have got well away on their road; they do not need to look back to origins. But sociologists have not got well away on their road.

The validation of induction gives us *terra firma*. But there is another aspect of this validation. It establishes limits to possible empirical knowledge. These limits are narrow, and probably much narrower than those impressed by the claims of the physical sciences appreciate. And so we come to my theme of 'this mysterious universe'. What, it will be asked, has this to do with sociology? The link is in the realm of the emotions. Understanding of the nature of our emotions is indispensable in the analysis of social relations. We shall be gravely handicapped, if not totally debilitated, if we try to formulate laws directly connecting impressions supplied to a person with his actions. The emotions are intermediaries, the existence of which it is fatal to ignore. Of course we can know about the emotions of other people only by introspection and analogy. The validity of all analogy is subject to logical tests.

The nature of our emotions will be modified by a continuing and heightened awareness of mystery. A given datum will not arouse the same feeling in one wandering in a strange and unknown country as would the same datum in one traversing familiar terrain. In fact we are all wandering in a strange country. The degree of appreciation of this fact varies from person to person. It must be a good thing to be reminded from time to time of such an important fact.

I suppose that an ego cannot postulate by analogy the presence of an emotion in other persons different in kind from any that he himself has experienced. But he can imagine an emotion of a given kind as being enlarged, even inflamed, in others, or, alternatively, as being present only in a weak form.

Whence can we get the best evidence about the pattern of emotions likely to be in people and inferable as present in them by inductive analogy? The sociologist is naturally especially interested in those affecting social relations. The best information is provided in the great creative works of literature, poetry and prose. That is a point on which I have been especially critical of Professor Homans in the fourth lecture. Not all creative literature provides such evidence, but much does. Its authors have been people with supernormal powers of understanding the pattern of human emotion in depth. Study of the great literature should have a leading role in any curriculum for students of sociology. In my original select list of three books, made when I began composing these lectures, I included *Bleak House*. I subsequently omitted it. Dickens was a mighty genius in his comprehension of human nature, but his work was rendered less than perfect by his cloying sentimentality, the boring nature of his 'good' characters, and the grossly exaggerated wickedness of his villains. My own inclination is rather towards the maxim, 'Tout comprendre c'est tout pardonner'.

Sociologists have got somehow to acquire deep understanding of emotional patterns, if they are to achieve work of any great importance. Where else acquire it but from the great literature? I am afraid that most of us just have not sufficient capacity to excogitate these things for ourselves.

Thus so far we have the supreme importance of the emotions in all social relations, and the importance of a sense of the mysteriousness of our universe in having an effect in conditioning our emotions.

In these lectures I have also dealt with ethics, laying stress on that branch of ethics constituted by moral codes. The place of morals within the wider area of ethics will be explained in due course. One could hardly have a worthwhile *general* treatment of sociology without a full discussion of ethics and morals; they may be quite important too for some specialised studies. Again I have found my thinking conditioned by a certain uneasiness about the present state of moral philosophy. This uneasiness also has continued for most of my life. When I was an undergraduate at Oxford, great stress was laid on intuition as the faculty that distinguished good from bad (in the ethical sense) and right from wrong. There was a parallel development of thought at that time in Cambridge under the influence of G. E. Moore. I always firmly rejected intuitionism. I have the impression – I hope that I am wrong – that there has since been a sort of downgrading of the importance of ethics and of moral principles. Some may even think that these subjects might well be allowed to disappear altogether. And then there has cropped up an expression that I particularly object to – 'value judgement'. For reasons that I shall explain in due course I just do not know what a value judgement is supposed to mean. But I have the feeling that the value judgements are supposed in some way to supersede the need for a soundly based study of ethics and moral codes. In my view the contents of these codes must be based on factual investigation and on reasoning of the highest quality and not on airy-fairy ideas.

This is a very complex and difficult subject, which intermeshes with social investigations of non-ethical matters.

As I am not a member of any church, I can only touch on the question of religion with extreme diffidence. It has clearly been a very important element and influence in human history. I do not think that this is just by accident and that we have here something that can be regarded as irrelevant, that can be forgotten about. Doubtless various religions have been replete with superstitions, and it is proper that we should want to get rid of these and put them into the waste-paper basket. But religion has been something more than a bundle of superstition, and something more than a collection of myths. I would not venture to attempt to describe the content of a pure religion stripped of superstition and myth. It is clearly a meeting-place of three of our topics — awareness of mystery, the pattern of our emotions and ethical codes. It may be that civilisation will proceed without the presence of any religion. I wonder.

I am convinced that moral suasion has a vital part to play in our society. This will be discussed in due course. We have plenty of moral suasion in our present-day society, but it seems to be ill-organised and not based on clear principles. Sometimes it seems to depend merely on the whims of individuals. The phenomenon of moral suasion necessarily involves an interconnection between the pattern of emotions and moral codes. One cannot persuade, unless one arouses some kind of emotion. Clearly not all persuasion can be classified as moral suasion; we may wish to persuade people about all sorts of incidental matters. Religious pastors, by the nature of their calling, could get a fusion also with our sense of mystery. Do we believe that what I might call purely secular moral suasion – by politicians, employers, etc. – will be effective?

I have tried to describe how the subjects of mystery, morals, economics and sociology, and also, although these subjects are not mentioned in the titles, inductive logic and the pattern of our emotions, intermesh.

1 Mystery

I MUST apologise for the subjects of these lectures being in the reverse order to their place in the general title; but this seems to make sense. The title should stress the subject-matter of the ultimate culmination. In the temporal order of events the valleys leading up to the culmination have to be explored first. I begin with a deep valley, which is a difficult approach. By its nature it will be, so to speak, the most solemn part of what I have to say.

It might be thought that a good showman should start with fun and games, lest his audience dwindle thereafter. Perhaps that would not be quite honourable. If there are to be fun and games in these lectures, this will presumably be when we come face to face with the question, is there something that can sensibly be called social science?

It is surely evident that we only know about a tiny bit of the great universe in which we live. Are we entitled to think that what we do know is a fair sample of what lies beyond? Are we even entitled to think that it is as likely as not to be a fair sample? I shall have something to say later today about a fair sample. I would suggest that we have no ground for supposing that what we know is as likely as not to be a fair sample. We have no ground for any view at all about what the disparity is between the bit with which we are acquainted and the general character of the wider sphere. I do not say 'the general character of the totality', because the notion of whole may not be legitimate.

If we ask what there is constituting the wider sphere, we

are enwrapped in mystery. A question more intimately connected with mystery is — W H Y? Why is what there is like it is? On the threshold of these speculations we are told that they are quite illegitimate. Speculations are allowed only in regard to matters where there is some prospect of success in answering the question raised. By what authority is this restriction imposed? I suggest that it is purely dogmatic. It is said by some that it is inherent in the meaning of the words 'thought' and 'inquiry' that they relate to matters where it is possible for questions asked to be answered. They put this forward as a definition of these words; a question has meaning only if the kind of phenomena constituting the answer to it, one way or another, can be specified in advance.

In the ordinary course of events, when we are not contemplating the mysterious universe, there are situations in which we may say 'We shall never know'. A headless human body is washed up on the seashore where there has been no record of shipwreck in a wide vicinity of space and time. One might wonder who the person was, being quite sure that one would never be able to find out. The objector might allow that such wondering was not absolutely senseless, on the ground that we might in principle know, that is, if we knew certain things that are in principle knowable. Wondering is ruled out by objectors of this kind if it is in principle impossible to find the answer. This attitude implies that it is possible to draw the line between what in principle can be known and what in principle cannot be known. The latter kind of wondering is ruled out. Why should there be this restriction on freedom? And is there a difference between what we shall in fact never know, but could in principle know, in which case wondering is allowed, and what we can in principle never know? One must have some doubts about that 'in principle'. The division between what is in principle possible and in principle impossible may change with the course of events.

I have the impression that the tendency to disallow wondering about what is mysterious is a manifestation of Puritanism. We should be forbidden to 'waste our time'. This may be a short-sighted view of the matter. Wonder about questions that can never be answered may have by-products that are enriching, e.g. in aesthetic creations or in subtle modifications of manners, the subject of my next lecture. Certainly social studies, if they are to lead to fruitful results, should be conducted against a background of wondering.

In the tendency to disallow wondering there may also be an element of inferiority complex. Problems that a human being cannot solve must be bogus problems. This is first cousin to

'What I don't know isn't knowledge'.

I come back to the word WHY? This question divides into what may be called material explanations (using 'material' in a wide sense) and explanations relating to purpose.

1. Material explanations in turn divide into

   (a) those relating a particular phenomenon to a known law or to known laws; or

   (b) those relating laws supposed to operate in complex specific areas to laws of more general domain.

For the former purpose one may examine phenomena in the vicinity. A man dies. There is an autopsy. Something in his body reveals that, by accepted physiological principles, it was practically certain that he would die. We have an answer to the question WHY.

In the latter kind of case there is the well-known trek from the laws of physiology, via chemistry, via biophysics, to pure physics. It is hoped that in the end the specific laws in all the particular sciences will be shown to be derivable from the laws of physics. The possibility of this reduction is not yet certain. Lord Cherwell, among his other great

intellectual gifts, had a genius for quantitative hunches –
a genius manifested in various contexts. I suppose that he had
an exceptionally efficient cerebral electronic computer. He
used to say that in the interval between the formation of the
solar system or, maybe, the first appearance of life on this
globe – the assessed intervals may have been changed since
then – there was just not enough time for random mutations
and natural selection to have produced the human body. In
that case we shall need some supplementary biological principles not deducible from physics to account for the phenomena.

Talking of the body, I often wonder, contrary to traditional doctrine, whether the human body is not a more
marvellous thing than the human soul.

A side comment may be permitted on the present state of
physics. Atomic physics seems to be in rather a ramshackle
condition. Departing from the old pair of proton and
electron, beginning with the neutron and culminating in the
neutrino, detectable only in deep goldmines in South Africa
and India, there has been a multiplication of ultimate particles within the atom, which, I am told, has accelerated
recently. This reminds one of the Ptolemaic epicycles of
astronomy in one period. We need a modern Kepler and
some new concept that will make possible a fresh model of
the atom on simpler lines than the present one. Of course
that would require a great genius and a prodigious effort of
thinking. An effort has been made in this direction by the
formation of the new concept of 'quark'. It is not yet certain
whether this will avail for reducing the basic concepts of
physics to better order.

It will be remembered that Newton, as well as doing
experiments, paced and repaced his study month after
month in a prolonged effort of thought. Has thinking
recently been going out of fashion? In economics certainly,
I would say, with due respect to my colleagues, that there

appears to be less thinking done than when I was young. I have the impression that designers of studies in modern universities pay no attention to the physical requirements for month-after-month thinking, simply because they have little idea of what thinking consists of. Thinking is, after all, more important than reading. I recall basing my programme for work, when I was an undergraduate studying Locke's *Essay Concerning Human Understanding*, on the plan that for every quarter of an hour of reading the text I should allow three-quarters of an hour for thinking about what I had read. The large glass windows, of which our architects seem so fond, are inimical to thinking. I remember A. N. Whitehead, who lived at that time in a conventional Victorian flat in Chelsea with quite modest windows, saying that, when he wanted to think, he always turned his chair with his back to the window. What would he think of our modern cubicles, with the whole of one side made of glass?

The working back from the more specific to the more universal, in answer to the question WHY, comes to an end if the laws of physics cover all phenomena within experience. Do they cover all phenomena? Specific biological laws may merely be a convenient shorthand for dealing with complex conditions and be ultimately inferable from physical laws. If material determinism governs all human behaviour – perhaps it does – it would be easier to predict conduct by the shorthand laws provided, doubtless, by sociologists, than by an exhaustive examination of the configuration of the atoms inside the brain and inferring what the body would do in consequence of that configuration. It is possible, however, that there are biological laws that exist, so to speak, in their own right, as suggested by Lord Cherwell, and are not deducible from the laws of physics. In that case there must at some point be a positive violation of the laws of physics. One cannot have it both ways. I waive this point for the time being.

Wondering still has a sphere. It is of course quite different from the Newton-type thinking to which I referred, but I believe that it is not, as some would hold, to be identified with mere wool-gathering. Why are there any atoms? Have they always been there? Why do they behave in the way that they do and not in some other way? This is a subject-matter of 'mystery'. At this point, the Puritans start up again. You are forbidden to let your wondering raise such questions, because they are in principle unanswerable. You cannot specify what researches you would put in hand in order to get an answer. Therefore you must stop this wondering.

What right have the Puritans to impose this veto? And can it here and now be absolutely certain that in this sphere of seemingly unanswerable questions there could never be any breakthrough?

2. Then there is the WHY relating to purpose. Why have I been provided with a platform on which to stand here? I cannot forbear another reference to university designers. In a new university I saw some very large lecture rooms without any platforms for the lecturer. Perhaps this was in deference to the principle of equality.

I need not elaborate on the many different kinds of questions relating to human purposes. We are used to asking the question WHY in many connections. Sometimes it turns out to be inappropriate, as when an arrangement was in fact designed by no one. Some objects that look as if they had been designed by someone as convenient benches on which to repose on the seashore may actually have been formed by the lapping of the waves. You must all have seen land formations that made you wonder whether they had been created by agriculturists of an earlier generation or were natural phenomena, perhaps caused by glacial erosion.

So one wonders about purpose in various connections and asks why — was there a purpose and what was it? And then one may ask the formidable question, did someone invent these atoms and endow them with their rather peculiar qualities, and why? The Puritans now approach their maximum of fury. You do not know of any such person. You could never find out by any known method of research if there was such a person. You are wasting your time by such wondering. I continue to wonder. Why do the atoms have the properties that they do have and not some quite different properties? We are no longer in the position where we were when we sought to explain certain laws governing chemical objects by inferring them from more general physical laws. With the atoms we have come to the end of that process, but not to the end of the urge to ask — w h y? We have come to the very heart of mystery.

One may wonder whether by intellectual effort one could reach the position of saying that, if something exists, it must have a certain property. Then one could go on from there and put the whole universe on a rational basis. But this would be contrary to the now generally accepted principle that about the whole universe of physical — should I say sensible? — objects nothing can be known *a priori*. If that is so, further wondering and asking why about the atom is fruitless in relation to obtaining an answer. None the less the wondering may be justifiable.

I turn to a rather different topic. I remember that, when I was quite a young child, my mother, who had lost or was losing her dogmatic faith, drew me to her in rather a solemn way and expounded the mysteries of infinite time and space. I do not suppose that she knew about the infinite series of natural numbers. This latter does not seem to cause the same intellectual tension as the infinitude of time and space. I think that I understand the reason why. It is true that numbers of fairly low magnitude are presented to us in our sensible experience; we validly can, and our forebears did, compose a multiplication table from sensible experience without any reference to ultimate definitions or axioms of mathematical logic. But the logicians have been able to derive from their definitions and axioms a schema which has a 1:1 relation with the mathematics of our sensible experience; then they go forward and handle infinite numbers in a valuable way, so I understand. They have thus made themselves independent of the sensible world; and their success in handling infinite numbers does not give us a headache.

The same cannot be said of time and space. In the case of time I have always found the backward extension more difficult than the forward one. Why should it not go on and on and on? But, if it has already been going on for an infinite duration, how has it managed to get as far as us?

It has been put forward that the universe consists of a space–time continuum of finite extent. I do not know how this stands at present, as I have not been reading in this subject very recently. The intermeshing of space and time is intelligibly explained in Einstein's special theory. For the finite universe we need, if I understand aright, his general theory, which is more speculative than his special theory. If you ask what is beyond the boundary of the finite universe, the answer is that there is no beyond; because of its curvilinearity there is no ultimate edge; there is no place at which there could be a beyond outside it. Is time looked after in this way? Could we not go on buzzing round and round for ever inside the space continuum? Presumably the intermeshing of space and time calls a halt to the infinite continuance of time also. I have never found anyone who could explain this to me satisfactorily.

And I am not convinced that this physical construction has solved the mystery of infinite time and space.

Nor am I content with Kant's solution of postulating that time and space are purely subjective, and categories that our mind has to impose on sensible phenomena before being able to perceive them. In his scheme they have no objective existence. I recall how one day in 1919 J. B. S. Haldane burst in among us at New College with an expression of great joy on his face: 'Einstein has proved scientifically that Kant was right', he said. During an eclipse, light rays had been seen to deviate accommodatingly towards the sun and this tended to confirm Einstein's hypothesis of curvilinearity. It was rather touching that Haldane, who later in life, particularly under the influence of his wife, became rather a Bolshy, in fact for a time a Communist, should have been so pleased about Kant. In the Oxford of 1919 Kant was a much revered philosopher, and Haldane had sufficient local patriotism to be pleased that his view should have been confirmed by the behaviour of the light rays.

Having mentioned Haldane, a very distinguished person, I should like to call attention to one of the very few errors, perhaps the only error, that I have been able to detect in Sir Maurice Bowra's superb autobiography. He gives a thumbnail sketch of Haldane, which is very true to life, except for the first sentence of it: 'Haldane was already a man of the left.' I recall Haldane's saying to me at that time: 'It may seem very old-fashioned to say so, but I regard the supremacy of the British Navy as a much more important contributor to the future peace of the world than the League of Nations.' Even in those days that was not a very left-wing sentiment. I recall another incident. He was an officer of the Oxford University Liberal Club. By chance at a meeting, its committee arranged itself in a semicircle around the fireplace in such a way that the left-to-right order of seating almost exactly reflected the left-to-right order of our political opinions. Haldane was sitting about in the middle, and pointed out the correspondence between seating and political opinion, thereby proclaiming himself a middle-of-the-road Liberal.[1]

[1] For non-British readers, it is expedient to point out that the British Liberal Party was itself a middle-of-the-road party. Its members were thus unlike those who would have been called liberal in the United States at that time

I am not convinced that either Kant or Einstein have dissolved the mystery of the infinite extension of space and time. It is a mystery about which we ought often to wonder.

Although it is out of fashion, I often meditate upon the views of Berkeley, a greater philosopher, I would suppose, than Kant, although not nearly so highly esteemed in the Oxford of 1919. One way of expressing his views is to say that, if there were no consciousness, there would be nothing at all. What, by some other view, would there in fact be? Just those atoms whirling around, unaware of their own existence and with no one else aware of them – whirling around in what one may call an outer darkness, and for all time.

Talking about a darkness, I recall going in a bell deep down into the Caribbean Sea (on TV), and coming upon a great galaxy of brilliantly coloured fishes, very beautiful. The fishes were far too deep down for any daylight to penetrate. But their physical structure was such that they had to live thus deep; otherwise they would go pop. So the inhabitants of the bell with their lamp were the first people to have gazed on those colours. The colours had presumably for long existed in some sense, maybe for thousands of years. So this is rather an anti-Berkeley story. Why those colours? Doubtless science can explain. This is not a mystery, but only what one might call a sub-mystery, which scientific research can dissolve into the light of common day.

If, in the absence of consciousness, nothing would exist, how comes it that we have our perceptions that suggest that bodies external to us do exist? Berkeley's explanation was that the Almighty has arranged for us to have sensible experiences in a regular and continuing order, so that we may live our lives in a methodical manner, picking our way among our sensible experiences and relying on their not letting us

---

who were very much to the left, and unlike the liberals of continental Europe, who are extreme conservatives.

down. I confess that this hypothesis does not altogether appeal to me. But I think that there is deep mystery as regards the intrinsic nature of so-called material objects, which we would do well to speculate about.

I would add this. The highest flights of science do not profess to enable us to know anything about the intrinsic nature of the atoms. The various properties assigned by science to them are defined in terms, the meaning of which can be interpreted only by reference to the impressions on *us* conveyed by the recordings of photographic lenses and other scientific instruments. About the things themselves that cause these impressions we know nothing except that, if the things exist, they have properties mathematically correlated with the scientific readings.

And so we have a number of mysteries, converging perhaps into one all-embracing mystery. How came the atoms into existence, if they ever came into existence and have not existed for an infinitude of time? Why do they have the characteristics that they do have and not quite different characteristics? There is the mystery of infinite extension backwards and forwards of time and the infinite outward extension of space in all directions. If there were no consciousness at all in the universe, would there be anything? And what would be its nature? And what is the intrinsic nature of the postulated objects to which the laws of science relate?

It would be appropriate for a civilised man to wonder about these mysteries, even if such wondering produced no ulterior effects. With economic growth per caput we shall be able to have more spare time. We cannot and should not *all* be do-gooders *all* the time, and I am sure that our sociologists, whom I picture as listening to me from the touch-line, or maybe they are not, will testify that their behavioural analysis indicates that, if a group is given through economic growth x more units of leisure time, it will devote only $x - y$ more units of time, y being either great or small according to the circumstances of the case, to do-gooding. It is better — but I am using this tendentious word 'better' in advance of any explanation which will be given in my next lecture — to sit like a Zen Buddhist monk looking at the rocks in a pond of well-swept gravel meditating upon the mysteries than to sit watching the TV.

It is true that contemplation of mysteries can have no influence on behaviour to the extent that that is directly governed by an analysis of facts. But betwixt and between our analysis of facts and our conduct comes the realm of emotion. That supplements our analysis of facts in the matter of influencing what we do. Some religions, particularly the Christian religion, I would say — without, I hope, belittling other religions, which have their various characteristics—, have sought, by confronting congregations with the great mysteries, to stir emotions likely to lead to better conduct. Again this tendentious word 'better' without definition. That is reserved for the next lecture.

The presentation of the content of mystery in a way that arouses emotion requires a certain technique. I do not suppose that what I have uttered today so far has aroused any emotion in the breasts of any of you; and it certainly would not to do so in the man in the street. Some forms of beautiful poetry and fine prose are capable of presenting mystery in a way that arouses emotion; some forms also of ritual. The Church of England had luck in having had a new wave of inspiration in the sixteenth and seventeenth centuries, by consequence of which the English Authorised Version of the Bible is probably — I am subject to correction by you — the finest version of the Bible, including in this the original version also, that exists. And the Church of England *Book of Common Prayer* is sans compare. In using the word 'finest' I am referring back to my description of a certain sort of prose as capable of presenting mystery in a way that arouses emotion. There is a great poetical phrase in the English Authorised Version, which obliquely touches on mystery and cannot fail to arouse emotion: 'Thy faith hath made thee whole.' I happened to see a modified translation which read, 'Your implicit confidence has brought about a complete recovery'.

Most religions, including the Christian, have based themselves on a factual story; and this was needful, apart from other considerations, in order to bring home to the ordinary man the relevance to him of its presentation of mystery. As centuries have proceeded, doubts have been cast on the literal veracity of the various factual stories. Renan and Matthew Arnold both hoped that the Christian religion might play down its factual story in favour of the emotion-rousing mystery-content of what, through the ages, it had traditionally taught. These two men do not appear to have had successors in their way of thinking.

I have been told — these are matters on which I do not have extensive first-hand information — that in the structure of their ceremonies and in the use of texts there has been a tendency in the Church of Rome and other Christian churches to play down the emotion-evoking mystery element in the language and form of service and to emphasise the more matter-of-fact element. Could anything be more perverse and stupid? I would infer that the average level of intellect among the Christian clergy from the highest level downwards has, subject to distinguished exceptions, deteriorated from its level in the nineteenth century. It is to be hoped that our sociologists are examining the hypothesis of deterioration in this area and its influence on conduct among the main mass of people.

I now propose to avail myself of the licence allowed me by the Warden of All Souls to dwell for a time on the subject of logic.

Most of the substance of what I propose to say is to be found in my book on inductive logic. But I hope that today I may be able to achieve a more easily intelligible presentation.

If my views are correct, the substance of what I am about to offer will have to be repeated over and over again, so long as *Homo sapiens* survives; for it relates to the very essence of our thinking process.

I believe that induction is a valid thought-process. This, if true, is lucky, since, according to modern thinking, it is the sole source of information that we have about the nature of things. I have a slight inclination to think that deduction may have been too much downgraded. I am not entirely sure that it is impossible to gain constructive knowledge about things by deduction alone. I have come across problems in economics where this has seemed to be so. It may be that in the century ahead there will be some rehabilitation of deduction.

However that may be – and I think that deduction could only have this power in fringe cases – induction must be our primary tool for gaining knowledge about the world. In the very process of demonstrating its validity, we get a clear view of its limitations. If establishing its validity makes sense of how we go about extending our knowledge of the environment, getting a clear view of its limitations very decidedly enlarges the area of mystery around us.

I am entirely opposed to all forms of pragmatism. I do not think that William James or Ferdinand Schiller were very deep-thinking philosophers. One form of pragmatism suggests that we should just observe the procedures of scientists in their researches, and content ourselves with the idea that, since scientists have had such great successes, their procedures must not be subject to critical scrutiny. It is held that one can get no further than observe their procedures and assume them to be correct, and that it is vain to ask *why* their procedures turn out right. But if you do not know why their procedures are right, you cannot define the limitations inherent in those procedures. And hence you cannot get an adequate idea of the vast area of mystery.

Incidentally, the present-day procedures of scientists, however successful, are unlikely to provide clues about the essential nature of induction. The reason for this is that they start with a vast background of knowledge (or presumed knowledge). But *Homo sapiens* starts from total ignorance about all connections between items of experience. The central problem of inductive logic is how he can validly get from the state of total ignorance to the privileged position from which modern scientists start. Some authors, in describing the procedures of these scientists, have stressed the trilogy of hypothesis, deduction and verification. That may give an adequate sketch of how current work proceeds, anyhow in some branches of science. But this kind of method would get nowhere without extensive prior knowledge of an empirical kind.

Two very distinguished philosophers, who have in fairly recent times tried their hands at the problem of induction, Keynes and Carnap, have both relied on a modified form of Bayes' Law; and indeed this has for long been given pride of place as an instrument of induction. But Bayes' Law requires that the empirical premise or premises of a piece of inductive reasoning have initial prior probability. This is precisely what we cannot allow, if we start from *Homo ignorans*. Keynes' attempt to solve the difficulty by postulating a finite number of ultimate generator properties is generally recognised to have been unsuccessful. Carnap has a wider sweep, but unfortunately he abandoned the project of writing his second volume. It would have been incumbent on him to show there that his more ambitious method could in practice get us more than very, very microscopic degrees of probability for any empirical proposition, degrees of probability in practice so small as to be negligible. When I say very small I am thinking in terms of the order of magnitude of there being a one billionth chance that X is the case. I do not think that in a second volume Carnap could have got much further than that. But in practice we assume a higher degree of probability than that for what we expect to happen next.

That very great philosopher, David Hume – the greatest since Aristotle, should we say? – posed the problem of induction in an admirable manner, but he could not solve it. He had to relieve the mental tension thereby set up by a game of backgammon.

Philosophers have been struggling with it ever since. In the nineteenth century there was a phase of optimism, represented by such men as John Stuart Mill on the one hand and the probability theorists of the school of Laplace on the other. But their theories contained fallacies, which came to be recognised.

This recognition led to a mood of despondency, not to say despair. It was out of this, I suggest, that pragmatism was born. Stop trying to solve that problem! Content yourself with seeing what maxims of methodological procedure seem to succeed, and adopt them. After all, that problem, which has seemed so difficult and has taxed logicians for so many years, was a *bogus* problem. Again I think a touch of inferiority complex entered in. 'What I cannot solve is not soluble.'

At this point I ought to mention one who, within such reading as I have done in twentieth-century philosophy, has had the greatest influence on my mind, Jean Nicod. He had no touch or trace of pragmatism and he rejected prior probability, but he thought that the central problem of induction was soluble, although he could not solve it. He had a hunch that what is known as 'the method of simple enumeration' was the most fundamental process in induction; that was sound. He died young, in the year 1923. Russell has told me that, among his former pupils, he regarded Nicod as a greater man than Wittgenstein. I have been at some trouble to organise a fresh translation of his *The Sensible Content of*

Geometry and the Problem of Induction from the French; this
is due to appear on 9 July 1970.

I should also mention Professor Donald Williams of Har-
vard University, who is not a pragmatist and believes the
problem to be soluble.

There lived for many years a few blocks away from here
a man who, after all, perhaps, we should rank above David
Hume, namely John Locke. He urged that, in trying to gain
understanding of the world, we should rely upon the principle of experience. If things within our experience have
behaved in a certain way, they may be relied on to continue
to do so. Two questions at once spring to the mind: (1) Why
should they continue to do so? Why should they not stop
doing so? (2) For how long will they continue to do so? For
ever? That would be rather a bold claim.

If things have gone on behaving systematically in a recognisable way for a substantial period of time, one might think
it unlikely that just at this present moment they would
suddenly stop doing so. 'Unlikely' is a word that requires
definition and it will shortly have it. It was a major flaw in
Keynes' *Treatise* that he postulated that its meaning could
be apprehended by intuition and that therefore it required
no definition.

Within our experience the sun has risen regularly each
morning. If it does not rise tomorrow morning, those of you,
if any, who survive, will comment that it was an extraordinary coincidence that the sun failed to rise on the next
day after a lecture by Harrod on the whole question of
whether the sun was likely to go on rising. As extraordinary
coincidences are much less frequent than non-coincidences,
you would be quite rational in laying a bet now that the sun
will rise tomorrow morning.

My wife, who knows little about equinoxes and solar
manifestations in the near vicinity of the North Pole, was
travelling over the North Pole some years ago. She was alone

owing to the fact that we had a rule not to fly together while our children were dependent upon us. She watched the sun setting amid a glorious blaze of gold and purple in the sky and on the ice. After sunset she turned to her book to fill the time before she felt sleepy. She had not yet begun to feel sleepy ten minutes later when she turned her head around and saw the sun rising in great majesty. Was this the moment at which the whole order of the world had changed? Or had she become mentally deranged? In due course she got a third explanation. But if her first hypothesis had been correct, she would have been perfectly entitled to be surprised, just as you will be if the sun does not rise tomorrow morning.

If one has been travelling over an area with specific characteristics, and is still doing so, one may frame the concept of its being of finite extent, although one does not know in the least what the size of that extent is. If the size of the area is infinite, as it may be for all we know – and in that case it will still be continuing long after we are dead – the argument that follows applies *a fortiori*. It will suffice for the moment to assume that the area began at the time when our personal experience of it began. Later we may learn that there are valid reasons, by inductive logic, for trusting historical records, e.g. about the rising and setting of the sun; but these reasons in favour of historical records can only be established after a great pile-up of evidence about various things long after man has ceased to be *Homo ignorans*.

By a purely intellectual process we are able to divide the continuum of continuingly similar specific characteristics into equal aliquot parts, without having any idea how large the continuum is. We can, for intsance, divide it into a thousand aliquot parts. If we survive the continuum, rather than the other way around – but my argument applies *a fortiori*, as I have said, if the continuum survives us – we can say that we shall have spent an equal amount of time on each of the equal aliquot parts, and that only one thousandth part of all our time will eventually have been spent on the thousandth aliquot part that immediately precedes its termination. From this I would suggest that at any time, if we know nothing about the extent of the continuum, there is only one thousandth chance of our being on the aliquot part which is the one thousandth aliquot part of the continuum immediately preceding its termination. It will, or should, occur to you that this is not quite correct, since we have already been occupying one, or possibly more, of the aliquot parts immediately adjacent to the beginning of the continuum. I will deal with that point presently.

I have been taken to task by the Wykeham Professor of Logic, who over the years has taken a kindly interest in my philosophical speculations, on the ground that my argument uses the illegitimate principle of equal prior probability, sometimes known as the principle of indifference. An example of that principle is as follows. If (somehow) it is known that there are only three colours in the world, say blue, red and yellow, and that everything in the world is coloured, and someone feels an object without seeing it, he may say that there is a one-third chance of its being blue. That would be quite illegitimate. The use of such a principle has been shown to lead to fallacies and contradictions. The spectator does not know the proportion of these colours in the universe nor the proportion in his vicinity nor what arrangement they have in his vicinity.

One comes a little nearer what is acceptable, but not all the way, if when one has a six-faced die which one (somehow) knows to have no bias, and a thrower whom one (somehow) knows not to be a conjuror, one says that there is a one-sixth chance of its showing a six.

My position is far stronger than that. It is analogous to the position of someone who knew for certain that on the first six throws a six would appear *once only* and then affirmed on the first throw that there was a one-sixth chance of the die showing a six. My position is actually stronger still. It is as though a six certainly would not appear more than once and might not appear at all, since the last aliquot part of the continuum might not appear in our lifetime, or, indeed, ever. One would say that there was *at most* a one-sixth chance of the six appearing and *at least* a five-sixths chance of its not appearing on the first throw. If the die had a thousand facets, and the same conditions applied, there would be *at least* nine hundred and ninety-nine chances to one against the 1000 facet appearing on the first throw.

The words probability, likely, *n*th chance, etc., have to be defined. I forbear to discuss the usage of some writers who have drawn a distinction between 'probable' and 'likely'. I am not sure if the Wykeham Professor has provided a definition. I suggest that *before* one has defined probability one can apprehend the nature of a situation in which one knows for certain that one will have for an equal time each of a thousand identical experiences, but has no idea which of those thousand the present one is. Will not this serve to generate a definition of probability? Let there be a situation in which we know for certain that we shall have a thousand experiences of equal duration and of character indistinguishable from one another, of which one experience has a character X which is entirely concealed from us, and about whose presence or absence we have not a clue. Let us agree to describe the character of the situation in which we are placed by saying that there is a thousandth chance of our present experience having the character X.

It may be objected that I have defined probability by reference to a particular type of case and that we need a more general formulation of the definition. That may be so. The advantage of defining probability by reference to a journey over a continuum is that this is the only case that I can think of in which the necessary conditions are fulfilled, namely that we know for certain that experiences of identical ostensible character will occur an equal number of times, that we know for certain that at most one of the experiences will have a concealed property X, and that we have no clue which of the experiences does contain this concealed property. It may be that we shall wish to apply the word probability, in an analogous sense, to situations in which the conditions are not so rigorously fulfilled. I would observe that in the history of philosophy, and of other disciplines, the root of the matter as regards some general relation has first been perceived in a specific instance of it. This perception in the specific case has inspired a more general formulation. I claim by my analysis of a journey over a continuum to have given you the root of the matter as regards the definition of probability and the validity of induction. It may be that someone will be inspired to do work to get a more general, but, I fear, necessarily looser, definition. But I give warning that the translation of my 'root of the matter' into a general formula would be likely (very loose use of that word!) to require many years of thinking.

I have still to clear up the point that our traveller over a continuum must have already been for a time in the first equal aliquot part of the continuum and may have been in more equal aliquot parts of it, and that this will diminish the proportion of time from a given point onwards that he will spend outside the terminal one thousandth aliquot part. We need to modify the definition of probability by making it represent the fraction of time that he will spend in the terminal aliquot part during what remains of his journey over the continuum. I have explained how this can be done in my book and illustrated it with a diagram. Taking all positions on the continuum, any one of which may have been overpassed at a given point of inquiry, we ask, as from *all* points on the continuum, what is the *average* ratio, as between the ratios estimated from each point on the continuum onwards, of true to false answers if the traveller states, 'I am on the last one thousandth aliquot part of the continuum'. Taking account of the positions already occupied in the past requires us to reduce the improbability of the traveller's being on the extreme edge of the continuum by about a half. But if the aliquot part used is quite small, it leaves a high probability for his not being on the extreme outer edge. I judge that this gives formal expression to Locke's maxim that we should trust to experience.

I remind you that the aforementioned calculation relating to the improbability of being on the extreme edge of a continuum is measured by reference to aliquot parts. We are all the time necessarily in ignorance of how many miles or years one aliquot part represents. As we proceed, the minimum *possible* value, in terms of years or miles, of a given aliquot part, e.g. a thousandth part, increases. Thus, if we can say that the probability of the pattern terminating before the end of the aliquot part which we are on is 1 in 500, the minimum value in terms of years or miles to which the improbability applies is continually rising. Thus, the longer the backward range of experience, the lower is the probability that the continuum will terminate tomorrow or next year or whatever the case may be. This gives a richer meaning to the maxim of Locke that we should trust experience.

If this is the correct logical validation of trusting to the principle of experience, it suggests that we can have a logical basis for prediction only for a limited period ahead. The size of this period depends upon the size of our previous experience. Pragmatists with their facile complacency do not tell us into how distant a future the successful methodologies of science can give us a view. The theory of valid induction provides us with a very definite answer to this. The further into the future that we seek to extend our view forward, the larger do we have to make the fraction constituting the aliquot part. The larger this fraction is, the less the improbability of our being on the terminal aliquot part. If we seek to extend our forward horizon, the perception of the objects on it becomes dimmer, and in due course all probabilities become minimal, tending towards zero. Beyond that we are faced, despite the wonderful achievements of science in relation to the present, with unfathomable mystery.

Locke's principle of experience in its simplest form, as I have tried to define it for you, takes *Homo ignorans* forward on his first steps to knowledge. As his knowledge increases, more complicated mental processes come into play. But the validity of these processes in every case rests on the validity of the principle of experience itself.

In the few minutes that remain I will confine myself to two subjects: sampling and simplicity.

1. *Sampling*. We may find that in our experience a certain characteristic A is always conjoined with B. That could happen, even if, in the region that we are exploring, not all A's are conjoined with B, or even if only a small proportion are. If we knew (which we do not) the proportion of cases in the whole population in the vicinity in which A is conjoined with B, we could work out what the fraction of all samples of a given size is in which A is always conjoined with B. We should have to deal separately with each size of sample. If in fact A is not often conjoined with B, there will be a far smaller fraction of large samples in which every A is conjoined with B than of small samples. No samples, however large, in which A is always conjoined with B can give us the certainty that in the whole population A is always conjoined with B. We can apply the notion of probability by assessing the fraction of samples, working separately for each size of sample, out of all samples of that size, in which all A's have B, on the assumption that in the whole population not all A's have B, but only 90 per cent, 50 per cent, etc. If it turns out that, on the basis of only 50 per cent of A's having B in the whole population, only in one millionth part of the

samples of this size do all A's have B and if in our sample all A's have B, we may argue that in the whole population in our vicinity more than 50 per cent of A's are likely to have B, and so on.

I have no intention of taking you into the intricacies. Time and again we may have bad luck and get a very unrepresentative sample. That is recognised by the fact that we only get probability, not certainty, by sampling, and that what is highly improbable may none the less be true. We have to face the fact that some samples may be very deceptive.

But we do work to the idea that we shall not continually be getting highly deceptive samples. We may express this by saying that while we are not unduly surprised by any one sample, e.g. of A having, or not having, B, being deceptive, we place confidence in the long run of samples of different properties, relating C to D, E to F, etc., being informative. Thus while we do not hope for each sample to be fair, we do hope that in our general experience the sample of samples that we get will be a fair one. We cannot, however, be sure of this. I doubt if we even have the right to think it probable. Professor Donald Williams, who has written authoritively about sampling, avers that, if the great majority of our samples are deceptive, there must be some wicked demon going about making them so.

I am not content with this, and believe that the difficulty, caused by our uncertainty about the fairness of our sample of samples, is resolved by the principle of experience. The unfairness of our sample of samples must have consisted either in making the world appear more uniform than it really is, or the other way around. We shall get the right result by assuming that our sample of samples is fair, as we normally do. The reason for this is that, if for a substantial time the characteristic of the region through which we have been journeying has been to provide us with a preponderance of samples leading us to infer that the world around us is more uniform than actually it is, we are not likely to be on the *edge* of a region in which that character of samples is maintained. If for a long time samples have been biased to uniformity, they will continue to be so for a forward period. If, by assuming our sample of samples fair, we have inferred a world more uniform than really exists, this will not lead us to make wrong predictions, because our samples – and it is only those with which we are concerned – will continue to show more uniformity than in fact exists in the world around. So if the outer world is not as uniform as our samples have suggested that it is and as we have inferred that it is and on that basis predicted that it will continue to be, we shall not be led into false predictions, because, by the principle of experience, our samples will continue for a time to show more uniformity than the outside world. It is improbable that we are on the extreme edge of a region in which samples are systematically biased towards uniformity. All this applies in reverse. The upshot is that we do not have to make an *a priori* assumption, which would not be justifiable, that our sample of samples is fair. The principle of experience relieves the validity of induction of any dependence on an assumption about the fairness of our sample of samples.

2. *Simplicity.* It is sometimes said, even by renowned theorists of scientific inference, that scientists assign higher *a priori* probability to simple laws of nature as against more complex laws, on the basis of an *a priori* probability that the character of nature is simple. That, if the case, would be abominable impudence. It would be as though someone from his own inner consciousness or prejudice began specifying the characteristics of the Deity. There is no *a priori* probability that nature is simple. But inductive logic gives *a posteriori* grounds for preferring a simple law.

We may suppose that it is desired to ascertain whether there is a functional relation between two or more properties.

If there is in fact no functional relation at all, none the less observations may be consistent with there being a functional relation. A random set of observations may show a relation, even if there would be found to be none if we had a wider set of observations.

Formulae may be ranked for their simplicity or complexity by reference to the number of adjustable parameters that they contain; the greater the number of adjustable parameters, the more complex the formula. The simplest formula of all is when the number expressing the amount of a certain property that a body has varies in direct proportion with the number expressing the amount of some other property. We can just say $x = y$, where x and y stand for the two numbers in question. A more complex formula would be $x = a + by^c$; here we have three adjustable parameters. Formulae can be devised with any degree of complexity.

If we take the case where there is in fact no functional relation between two properties, and we have a finite set of observations, we can always devise a formula of sufficient complexity, e.g. with as many adjustable parameters as we have observations, to make the observations conform to the formula. If in fact there is no functional relation, further observations would presumably show values for the properties not complying with the formula.

There are far more possible formulae of a given degree of complexity than there are possible formulae of a lower degree of complexity. Consequently, given that there is actually no functional relation between the properties, the number of sets of possible observations that would conform to one or other of all possible formulae of a given degree of complexity is far greater than the number of sets that would comply with one or other of all possible formulae having a lower degree of complexity. For instance, it might be that of all possible sets of observation, one in a thousand such sets would conform to one or other of all possible formulae of a given degree of complexity, while only one in a million such sets would conform with one or other of all possible formulae of a lower degree of complexity.

That is why, when confronted with a set of observations conforming to a simple law, I have much greater confidence that that law does actually operate to connect the properties than I would be if the set of observations conformed to a more complex law.

There is absolutely no trace here of any *prior* presumption that the laws of nature are more likely to be simple than complex. The greater confidence that I have, when confronted with phenomena that seem to conform to a simple law, that that law is actually operating, is deducible from sampling theory. We may add that if the laws of nature are in fact simple, they will be easier to discover with very high degrees of probability than they would be if they were more complex. Some parts or aspects of nature may be simpler than others; scientists will be able to make quicker progress in relation to the former. Sociologists beware!

Confidence in simple laws depends proximately on the assumption that our sample of samples is fair. But it does not, as we have already seen, depend ultimately on that, but solely on the principle of experience. If for a period our sample of samples has been biased towards making nature seem more uniform and simple than it really is, we are not likely at any point of time to have come to the end of that period. Since the phenomena with which we are confronted will continue for a time to show greater uniformity and simplicity than exists in nature generally, we may confidently predict that the relations that we have observed will continue to be manifested, but for a limited range only. Beyond that range, however beautiful the simplicity of the laws that scientists have managed to conjure up for us, we are enshrouded in unfathomable mystery.

2   Morals and Manners

'THOU shalt love thy neighbour as thyself.' Why should I do so? No set of facts can be specified from which, if they were true, this precept of conduct, which is what in effect it is, would follow as an inference. It is set forth in the imperative mood. Is there some more general precept from which it can be derived?

I suppose that a theologian might argue that it can be derived from the more general precept, 'Thou shalt obey thy Lord'. This does not appeal to me, because, by making this ethical maxim dependent on deeper mysteries, it seems to belittle its self-illuminating character. I use the word self-illuminating as the analogue in ethics of self-evident in the realm of factual matters. Of course we are told nowadays that nothing is self-evident. That need not discourage us. Perhaps the idea of self-illuminating was, wrongly or rightly, carried over from the mood of the imperative to that of the indicative, where, according to some, it has no place, and not the other way round.

We can have no *a priori* concept of the meaning of ethics. Accordingly I define it as the subject-matter of the study of all that follows from the 'love they neighbour' precept.

What is required by this precept corresponds roughly to the doctrines of utilitarianism. In the calculus of benefits and detriments, the self is to be reckoned on a par with others, neither more nor less important. As we have much greater knowledge about what gives the self pleasure than about what gives other people pleasure, and as the action by which a good can be obtained with high probability is, by common sense, to be preferred to one of doubtful accrual, the maxim may tilt matters somewhat towards self-interested conduct.

One can of course adopt a slightly different principle, whereby the self is to have no weight at all in the calculus of pleasure. This is an extreme position. One can think of utterly selfless people, rare perhaps, who devote their whole lives to promoting the good of others without a thought of self. By the strict utilitarian principle and by the literal wording of the 'love thy neighbour' precept, such people deviate from the proper line of conduct, whereby one's own pleasure is to be given on the scales exactly the same weight, neither more nor less, as that of other people. All the same, it seems to be in accord with the intention of the precept that those who love their neighbours more than themselves should not be regarded as deviating from it.

It has been held by some, notably in the last century, that if a man goes out of his way to help others, that must be because he gets more pleasure from doing so than he would get by equal effort in any other way. The doctrine is that the objective of maximising one's own pleasure is the sole ultimate determinant of all conduct. This proposition has no authority. It lies, not in the domain of ethics, but of psychology and could be rendered probable only by empirical investigation. While there is in many cases a happy consilience between giving the self pleasure and giving others pleasure, which is deeply rooted in human nature, the universal proposition that, whenever there is altruistic action, there is always such a consilience, i.e. that the altruistic action *must* give the self pleasure, is entirely unacceptable. One has seen many instances where it appears to be false. There is no *a priori* reason whatever for supposing that these instances are deceptive. It may equally well go the other way, namely that there is more genuine self-sacrifice than there seems to be on the surface. It is important to get this facile and cocksure generalisation out of the way. The foregoing question is entirely different from and independent of the question of determinism, whether determinism in the form of all actions being governed by the arrangement of material particles or of all being governed by psychical antecedents in accordance with some law.

I cannot mention utilitarianism here without thinking of that great man, who lived for many years in Chichele's college, Francis Ysidro Edgeworth. His reputation is still growing, and I should not be surprised if in the long run his place in history as an original thinker in economics overtops that of Alfred Marshall, who during their lifetimes was so much more famous in what it is now fashionable to call this 'offshore island'. A popular expression at one time for describing the objective of utilitarianism was to get the 'greatest possible happiness of the greatest possible number'. I remember Edgeworth observing with some scorn that this was as though we said that we wanted the greatest possible illumination from the greatest possible number of lamps.

He may have felt annoyed because he thought that the popular phrase was twisting the pure doctrine of utilitarianism in an egalitarian direction. Spread the butter more widely, even if you thereby reduce the total amount of butter and the sum total of human happiness. But I believe that he was thinking rather of the population question, to which the expression is clearly relevant. It is a difficult one to handle, because the ninth baby may have a happier life than any of the other eight. One may take a wider sweep and consider whether, if one increases the population of an overcrowded region by 1 per cent, one thereby causes the lives of 1 per cent more people than would otherwise be the case to contain no positive net content of happiness at all. If that happens, the increase of population would not comply with the tenets of utilitarianism. One can go further. Even if the lives of the marginal 1 per cent do have some positive net content of happiness, their presence is not desirable if it causes a decline in the aggregate happiness of the remaining 99 per cent by an amount greater than the sum total of the happiness of the extra 1 per cent. He did not go further than this and propose, as some selfish affluent members of society might like to think, that any population increase that diminished average happiness was undesirable. If the aggregate happiness of the marginal 1 per cent was greater in sum than the loss of happiness of the remaining 99 per cent, then the increase was in accordance with utilitarianism.

I am afraid that these considerations imply the validity of cardinal measurement, which is out of fashion nowadays. It is rather fascinating that Edgeworth, who was the inventor, and acknowledged as such by Pareto, of the indifference curve, so popular now, and rightly so within its limitations, would not agree that it enabled one to dispense with the need for cardinal measurement in many cases. I heard him arguing vigorously on more than one occasion that it was possible to have interpersonal comparisons of pleasure.

The precept that I set forth at the outset of this lecture is of a very general character. What to do to fulfil it? Both the words 'love' and 'neighbour' may mark a difference between it and the more abstract maxims of altruism. There are two separate points: (1) One is that, if we subscribe to the precept, even if only in theory and not, owing to weakness, or not fully, in practice, we presumably wish others to do likewise. That seems to follow. If people are to shape their conduct by a precept, it should have some emotional backing. You are more likely to do the things prescribed if you actually feel love for the people. Love provides the motive power. 'Neighbour' may also be relevant. It is more difficult to have real love, apart from lip-service, for remote people whose characters are unknown to you.

(2) Secondly there is the question of what in particular ought to be done. That is a very difficult question. Love and

vicinity may both provide clues as to what is really needed, and generate more effective altruism than would otherwise be obtainable. Of course love may take a wrong turn, as in the case of the possessive love of some parents.

But, when all is said and done, we need a systematic study of our complicated social structure and the interconnections of its parts, to ensure that a seemingly kindly act will not do more harm than good in the long run. 'Spare the rod and spoil the child.' It is the task of sociologists to get an ever deeper level of understanding of the interconnections in terms of ways of life, economics, environment and above all of the emotional content of various social relations, being a boss, a middleman, the lowest-paid type of employee in a factory, etc. In seeking criteria for assessing the content of effective altruism, we need to peer as far as we can into the future, so as to trace the distant ramifying effects of an action. This is said to be becoming more difficult nowadays owing to the increased pace at which economic and social arrangements are changing.

May I be permitted a digression? The aphorism that I used just now may have been displeasing to the ears of some modernists. 'Spare the rod and spoil the child.' I did not use it with malice propense, but because it seemed the shortest and most epigrammatic way of expressing the idea that I had in mind, namely the possible contrast between the effects of bene-volence in the short term and those of benevolence having regard to the more remote consequences of the action.

I happen to believe that the maxim quoted is correct. I believe that discipline is very important for the young child and that the absence of it at that crucial age may have a very bad effect on psychical stability in later years. The human emotional complex needs to be confronted even at three years of age with a life that has a definite form and insistent pattern. One needs something to bite on that is real. In the nature of things a young child's life can have no natural pattern forced on it by the structure of what he confronts. He can play around with his toys, and get bored. Accordingly it is incumbent to impose an artificial pattern, consisting of rules that may have no great value in themselves – but may even have that in relation to the comfort of adults – and to enforce those rules, if necessary. Naturally I am not condoning brutal treatment that may leave permanent scars; but a thorough spanking is normally harmless enough.

The absence of a definite pattern, in fine of discipline, leaves an emotional vacuum. And this, I feel confident, is bad in the long run for health. I believe that the more permissive attitude to children was started in the United States under the influence of false psychology; it has come here. I may be wrong, but I have a hunch that this permissiveness is one factor responsible for the adolescent and adult lawlessness that has been growing. I hope that sociologists are investigating this hypothesis.

To return to the main theme, the content of ethical codes should depend on an analysis of causation in social relations. This is a complex matter. The chains of causation are long and the interplay of social relations is intricate. Only by an understanding of them can we validly fill out the content of ethical codes. This statement would have given great offence to another near neighbour of Chichele's college, F. H. Bradley. He regarded discussion of the detailed content of codes of conduct with great contempt, excluding it from the subject of ethics proper and relegating it to the topic of 'casuistry'. But then, what is left for ethics? When one has said, 'Thou shalt love thy neighbour', what more is there to be said, if one does not analyse specific situations?

The *moral* code is one part of the wider ethical code. It is something that is insisted on with greater strictness, and such words as 'duty' and 'obligation' and, when there is a violation, 'wrongful act' become applicable. It is considered a good thing to be altruistic, whenever, and as much as, possible. But it is not considered a binding duty to be altruistic on all occasions. With morality, the case is, or anyhow has been considered through most of recorded history to be, different. Words like 'duty' and the others need definition. Their meaning is not supplied *a priori*.

I believe that Kant, whose views about time and space I rejected in the last lecture, has given us the most satisfactory explanation of this matter. The question of whether a certain line of action is a duty or, alternatively, a wrongful act, arises when it is pertinent to ask the question, what would happen if everyone, or many people, in identical relevant situations did (or did not do) the thing in question? There are frequent cases when, if I do not do a certain thing, no foreseeable harm on an objective estimate can come to me or anyone else — thus abstention from doing it does not seem to violate the general principles of altruism — but when, if many others in identical circumstances do not do it, great harm comes. We have a situation analogous to that well known in economics of 'increasing returns to scale'.

Truth telling is probably the best example of a moral obligation. I will return to 'white lies' and 'mercy lies', which are exceptions, presently. A case may arise in which I can foresee a little gain to myself, and no possible harm to anyone else, if I tell a lie. On a strict utilitarian calculus, the lie would even be desirable as tending towards the greatest pleasure. But then it might be that, if everyone with no more inducement than I have, told the lie, this would seriously undermine confidence in the veracity of human communications. Just my telling the lie on the occasion referred to would not have this tendency, especially if no one knew that I had told it. But, if the habit became general, its existence could not fail to become known. Habits generally prevalent cannot be kept entirely secret.

Any undermining of confidence in veracity would have a disastrous effect. Indeed, if the matter went far enough, we could no longer maintain in being the kind of society that we have. I believe that this condition does obtain in some primitive communities; this would be an important cause of their remaining primitive; doubtless there is action and reaction.

In societies tinged with the doctrine of altruism the spiritual mentors and public opinion tend to keep things going by making citizens feel their pleasure or displeasure at what is done. Violations of moral laws incur much more stern displeasure than does a mere selfish neglect of altruism. It is unlikely that many, if any, custodians of morality explicitly understand the Kantian principle. None the less they have and express abhorrence at a violation of the moral code. They may be influenced by tradition or by religious codes. The evolution of moral codes has proceeded through many centuries of history. It is to be hoped that sociologists never let go far from the forefront of their minds the vital role played by tradition and the extent to which any kind of good society must depend on it. There may have been important occurrences of sudden change, *seisachtheiae*, when, things being in a rotten state, it has been decided to root out practices like fraud and bribery, and, when the outcome was satisfactory, the remedial maxims were handed down as rules that must be obeyed without fail. Finally, it is possible that, although the mentors would not recognise the formal explanation of Kant, they do understand at a deeper level of consciousness the essence of his principle.

The most notable example of 'mercy lies' is in the case of mortally sick patients. Such lies do have an effect on a doctor's credibility. But it is probably more comforting to be told 'You will recover', even though you know that the doctor may be telling a mercy lie, than to be told 'You cannot recover'. (I do not profess to know what the most modern medical practice is in this matter.)

The principle applies in similar cases. If it is established that the loss of credibility due to its being known that lies are often told in a certain type of case does not matter very much, then the stern veto can be relaxed, but only in that type of case.

'White lies' belong perhaps to my theme of 'manners'. But I shall discuss them right away.

Lies may be called white when they are told within strictly limited areas, generally recognised by a society, in which the consequent loss of credibility does not matter much. One goes into a painter's studio and, looking at one of his products, says 'What a fine picture!' The painter thinks, 'He is only saying that to be polite'. A lie told within such an area does no damage to one's general reputation for veracity. One may not be a good judge of painting, or not in all cases, and, if this were such a case, the pain given by what one believed to be the truth would not be accompanied by any compensating advantage. If the painter is really incompetent, he will discover that in due course by the failure to get many commissions. There are, it is true, some people who take pleasure in saying what they really think on such occasions; one does not usually like such people.

In the old days when maidservants were abundant and dropping in more frequent, if one did not want to be interrupted by a caller, one told the maid to say that one was 'not at home'. This was within the recognised area of white lies, and the statement therefore lacked full credibility. But it was open to the caller to think, 'Well, perhaps, he really isn't at home'. It was better than saying, 'He is at home, but is too busy to see you'.

That reminds me of a sad incident, told me by my mother. Algernon Swinburne was for many years a great friend of my grandparents. They had numerous children and consequently a large luncheon table. Friends, including Swinburne, often dropped in and partook of lunch. On one occasion he arrived completely blotto. My grandmother took him into the drawing room and made him repose on a sofa there. Soon afterwards he fell off it with a loud thud, clearly audible to the children around the lunch table. My grandmother told the maid, 'If Mr Swinburne calls again, say that we are not at home'. The sofa in question is still in use in my drawing room.

Keeping a promise is another leading case of moral law. Faith in promises, which is a very important element in the functioning of our society, would seriously wane if it was known that people would break their promises, whenever it appeared that by an objective calculation on strict utilitarian principles of the present and remote effects of breaking a particular promise there would be no net loss of pleasure. It is absolutely necessary to re-do the calculation on the basis of everyone breaking a promise in precisely similar relevant circumstances. Although there might be no resulting loss of pleasure to anyone in each particular case taken separately, there could be a grave loss of pleasure if it were known that promises would be broken in all such cases, since the consequent loss of confidence in promises as such would be gravely detrimental to the efficient conduct of business, in industry, commerce, politics and other important spheres. Indeed one can go further and say that there could no longer be any such thing as a meaninfgul promise.

I recall Frank Ramsey, a philosopher of the highest distinction, who died young, elder brother of the present Archbishop of Canterbury, coming to stay with me at Christ Church, and my taking him to the Philosophical Society to hear the late Professor Paton, then tutor at Queen's, read a paper on moral obligation. There was an active discussion in which Ramsey did not take much part. 'Why', he remarked to me indignantly afterwards, 'did they discuss morality in terms of such a boring subject as keeping promises, instead of dealing with something interesting like fornication?'

Murder is to be condemned both by the principles of

general altruism and by morality. One could hardly do anything more anti-altruistic than terminating for ever a source
of feeling in the form of a person destined to carry through
time a net balance of happiness. It is also important – this is
the moral side – that people should be trained by tradition
and the suasion of moral mentors to view murder with great
abhorrence, so that, when provocation reaches boiling-
point, they should be restrained, not only by the danger of
punishment, but also by emotional abhorrence; otherwise
murders would be more frequent and ordinary people
would go about in greater fear of their lives. A grave detriment. In a tiny way this is already happening in some
American cities.

Keeping the law, even in cases when violation cannot be
found out, is another example of moral obligation. While
there are doubtless many people who find means of evading
the law – this means breaking it – there remains a great
majority of steady-goers who do their duty in this respect.
Without them it would be much more expensive to maintain
the law, and even impossible.

Of course there may be periods of very bad government
with laws in operation widely deemed to be detrimental,
when the citizens decide that their duty to obey the government lapses. This is traditional liberal doctrine. If there is a
widespread refusal to obey any longer, then there will be
some upheaval, some breakdown of the system of government as it is at the moment, in fine a revolution, whether
bloodless or violent.

In such circumstances, it would not be correct, according
to Kantian principles, for an individual to argue that, as the
government was rotten and the laws vile, he no longer felt
at a moral obligation to obey, when he could disobey without
being found out. Of course, if he were found out, he would
be in for trouble on ordinary utilitarian principles. What he
must assess on Kantian principles are the consequences of

his and all other individual victims of the bad laws ceasing to obey them. In fine he must assess the turmoils due to a general revolution against the benefits likely to flow from a new and better government. The latter in turn depends on what chances there are of getting a better government after a period of turmoil. As such matters are uncertain in the extreme, there is a case for the moral mentors of society emphasising the duty to obey the laws, however bad, and to have patience. None the less in the end Kantian principles may justify a revolt.

Without, I hope, seeming to brag, I think that I may say that I have always been a faithful law-abider. Perhaps I ought to announce, on the occasion of this Chichele Lecture, that I might have doubts about my unquestioning duty by Kantian criteria to obey legislation emanating from Brussels.

In the case of truth telling there is little doubt of the result one would get if one supposed everyone to lie when no harm in the particular case could be foreseen. The likely outcome of law-breaking is not always so clear. Doubtless there are many other cases, subject to a moral code, where one cannot see what the result would be if everyone violated the code in certain circumstances. It may be a very subtle matter. One may have to trust to 'hunches', and the hunch of the wise man may be better than that of the other fellow. There is still a role for wisdom, the computer letting us down.

In my undergraduate days, the prevailing view in Oxford was that judgements about right and wrong were a matter of direct intuition. There was a certain ethical quality in this action or that, it was held, which could be directly observed. I regard this doctrine as totally unacceptable. It is not to be confused with my doctrine for the need of a 'hunch' on certain occasions and the role of what is called wisdom. In the case of lying, there is no question of its having a certain innate intuitable quality. It is a question of *fact* how much detriment would be done if lies were always told on a certain type of occasion. In borderline cases it may be mightily difficult to make the assessment. That is where we have to fall back on the wise man's hunch. A computer could *in principle* solve the problem. But it is quite impossible to give it the necessary data.

Frank Ramsey wanted to hear more about fornication. Sex is a very difficult subject. I confess that from my early days I thought that the code, anyhow as formally purveyed at that time, namely that there should be complete continence save between spouses, was insufficiently permissive. I extended my tolerance to homosexuality. The formally accepted code has been changed since then – on the whole, I believe, for the better, for reasons on which I need not expatiate.

Principles of sexual behaviour used to be put forward as part of the general moral code; but there was this difference. Whereas most ordinary decent people were not frauds, cheats or thieves, conformity with the code of sex morals was much less widespread. This gave grounds for thought.

I believe that the sex standards are related to all three divisions of my subject today, morals, altruism and good manners. On the last of these I have hardly touched, as yet.

On the side of morals, Hume made the most important contribution. He drew a distinction between the complete chastity – subject to marriage rights – expected of women and a more relaxed attitude as regards men. This largely corresponded with actual conduct over many generations. It is not, I fear, congenial to the sentiment of equal rights for men and women. He held that fathers ought to be able to have grounds for complete confidence that their so-called children were in fact their own, so as to give them a human motive to work hard for their benefit. That the fathers should have this motive for doing so was good, not only for their children, but for society as a whole, by keeping it industrious. To secure this unqualified confidence, it was needful that most women should have complete abhorrence for extra-marital relations. Thus, as regards the determination of standards of feminine conduct, it was not enough that a woman should be able to say, 'I can keep this secret; accordingly it will give my husband no pain and me pleasure'. That suffices for the utilitarian calculus. For the Kantian principle she must also ask, 'What would happen if all women with no greater temptation than I have were unfaithful?' This would hardly fail to undermine confidence in female chastity; a particular case could be kept secret, but a general habit could not be.

It may be consistent with Hume's doctrine that over some centuries – sociological historians must correct me if I am wrong – ladies in the higher ranks of life were more lax in their behaviour than others. *Their* children would be all right anyway, and there would be no need for their father (or putative father) to toil and moil on their behalf. What is the position at present? What fathers can do for children is much more limited than it used to be, both because of state aid and because of death duties. I shall return to that point.

I suppose that a corollary of Hume's ethic is the social acceptance of professional prostitution. When I went up to Oxford, there was at least one college, not mine, at which freshmen could expect to find on their desks, presumably put there by a second-year man or an official of the Junior Common Room, some convenient and safe addresses, safe in the sense that one was unlikely to pick up venereal disease there. Such a method of disseminating desired information by an office routine was much more civilised than an approach on the lines of 'Hey, boy, I can tell you something'. I feel confident that there is no such routine at any college now.

Sentiment has changed. There is now the feeling that in early extra-conjugal relations, it is seemly that there should be some sense of affinity, not amounting to love in the full and proper meaning, but sufficient to enable the partner to kid himself with the idea that he was a little bit in love. Of course, if we look at the matter in terms of the summation of pleasure, it may be that there are many, including superior persons, who get more satisfaction from plunging into a carnal act and concentrating on that, without having to have their heads bothered by the irrelevant idea of being a little bit in love. For them prostitution may be suitable. It is for psychologists, by factual investigation, not from their own prejudices, to determine the ratio of those who get more satisfaction from one type of sex activity to those who get more satisfaction from the other.

Our modern attitude may, paradoxically, have reduced the average amount of carnal intercourse. The effects of this, if any, on physical and mental well-being are a matter for study. I doubt if they are of quantitative importance.

To revert to conjugal fidelity. Straight altrusim also provides an argument for it. In most cases infidelity, if not kept strictly secret — and to do so might involve lies and deception — is likely to cause more pain to the injured spouse than pleasure to the unfaithful partner. This point does not bear upon pre-marital relations.

I next come to a point that relates not so much to conduct, although it could have some bearing on that, as to general attitudes. There appears to me to be a tendency currently to stress the allurements of sex. Walking through the London Underground one sees far more sexy pictures than one used to. I am told that it is the same if one goes to the theatre. This must surely be in accordance with what people wish and are prepared to see. Why not? Display of what is sexually alluring may give pleasure, especially to those who have not found a regular manner of sufficient sexual satisfaction.

It strikes me that this tendency to publicise and implicitly stress the importance of sexual allurement is very ill-mannered to ugly people. I would go further and express my belief that age-old traditional codes of reticence in relation to sexy matters have been built up as a form of politeness to the ugly.

I am not suggesting that the latter do not achieve their fair share of sexual satisfaction. We see lovely girls marrying hideous men and conversely; the marriage market does not suggest that the ugly are necessarily at a handicap; and what has sex appeal differs widely from person to person. Still, there must be some sense of being a little out of it on the part of the most manifestly ugly people. To go about and beat on a drum crying loudly 'Sex appeal is what matters most' is definitely rude to them.

There was a doctrine strongly held and forcefully expressed in my youth that true love was much more important than sex attraction. That was correct doctrine, since true love, but hardly sex allurement, can bring happiness for a lifetime. And it was good manners vis-à-vis the ugly, since it prevented their feeling debarred from the delights that mattered most.

I cannot refrain from calling attention here to what seems to be a contradiction. One on side of the moving stairs in the underground there are pictures of ladies rather starkly conveying sex allurement of an age-old traditional type. On the other side are live beings in motion, upwards or downwards as the case may be, male, who appear to be concealing under fungus and filth any vestige of sex appeal that they may have.

The other day a very charming young man, not filthy and ill-kempt, but dressed in the most fantastic and ornate apparel, observed to me that he regarded 'making one's exterior look as one liked as a fundamental human right'. I was not quick enough to reply that I did not believe in the existence of such things as 'fundamental human rights'. I am rather doubtful about the meaning of the word 'right' in common usage apart from legal rights. Presumably one has a right not to have a wrong inflicted on one – a right, for example, to be paid debts due. Has one a right to do anything that one likes that is not wrong? There is the borderline region of altruism. Presumably one would be said to have a right not to be altruistic at all times whenever occasion offers. But I think that by common usage one would say that X had no right to lead such an atrociously selfish life as he did, although he complied with all moral obligations.

As regards external apparel, altrusim would suggest getting oneself up in the way that gave greatest pleasure to those who saw one. But perhaps my young friend was correct in saying that he had a 'right' not to do so. I would not, however, be disposed to grant him a 'fundamental' right.

I judge that the word 'wrongful' has a somewhat wider coverage in ordinary usage than 'immoral' in the Kantian sense. While we do not say that there is a duty to give pleasure on every possible occasion, we may say that it is wrongful to give pain unnecessarily, not by application of the Kantian principle, but taking each case separately. There seems to be an asymmetry here. Can we say that there is a self-illuminating imperative condemning the infliction of n units of pain more strongly than the failure to convey n units of pleasure, even although the two packets weigh the same on a pair of utilitarian scales and, taken together, are on the indifference curve of an individual? If so, perhaps, after all, those who attire themselves in a hideous manner may be regarded as wrongdoers.

On manners Oscar Wilde's aphorism surely has the palm. 'A gentleman is a person who is incapable of giving pain unintentionally.' I happened to mention this not long ago to a person of great culture and literary renown and, incredible as it may seem, he replied, 'Oh, but surely was it not —' (I forget the name of the person, Cardinal Newman? Bishop Creighton?) 'who first defined a gentleman as a person incapable of giving pain?' He had missed the point of 'unintentionally'. Without it, the definition is, first, clammy, and, secondly, utterly false. Gentlemen are quite capable of giving pain intentionally, right, left and centre, and often do.

How avoid giving pain unintentionally? One has to understand general human nature at a deeper level than can be conveyed in textbooks or treatises. And one has to understand the specific sensitivities of the person before one. If one is to be 'incapable' of giving pain, one has to want to understand them and be capable of doing so. For some, an inner core, this has come through childhood training. Some parents elevate good manners into being the first commandment in the moral code. The child can watch in action the quick appreciation by adults of the sensitivities of other people. The subject is a fascinating one. Indeed for one not aspiring to the higher flights of mathematics or music, it can be the most interesting one in life. And anyone who feels that he knows something of the art of not giving pain unintentionally will want to practise it. I am not denying that, none the less, many louts and boors come out of gentle homes. And, of course, Wilde's gentleman is an ideal; he does not exist in the flesh.

I shall take as my leading theme in what follows the question of equality. You may recall that so far my main specific illustration of good manners related to inequality of pulchritude. I picked up this horrible word from an obituary notice of an aunt of mine in *The Times*, which said that she was a person of supreme pulchritude. So indeed she was! I suggested that good manners, as embodied in a recognised pattern of comment and attitude, would be to belittle the importance of sex allure in the general scheme of things, so as to make ugly poeple feel more comfortable. It would be absurd to suggest abating praise of beautiful people; indeed the ugly should be invited to join in; that is itself part of good manners. So inviting them is a sign that we think that they know that we know that external beauty is not of all that importance in relation to the deeper currents in human affairs. And we can joke with them about a pretty woman having got away with something quite unjustifiably. How monstrous of her!

There are inequalities right across the board of human characteristics. It may be pleasant to suppose that if an individual, A, was inferior to B in respect of one characteristic or many, this would be compensated by superiority in other respects, so that, overall, individuals were equal one with another. This would be by an unlikely coincidence. We have to recognise that people are in fact unequal on overall average in their qualities.

Doubtless there is some almost mystic respect in which we like to think of all men as being equal. In religious terms some might express this by saying that they are equal in the eyes of God, or, again, that their inequalities are so trivial by comparison with their inferiority to Him as to be negligible. In human terms there is, I believe, something genuine in our sense that there is truly an equality of some kind. I have tried to think how to express this. The best that I can do to try to express what we mean is to say that all human beings should have equal consideration. Therein is constituted what might be called the brotherhood of man.

The main cause of difference of characteristics is, I do not doubt, genetic difference. One has only to compare the vast differences between brothers, born very closely after one another into an identical environment, to be convinced of the importance of inherited characteristics. In my reading in this subject I have been much influenced by the work of R. A. Fisher.

The environmental influences divide into what, without self-contradiction, we may call those of hereditary environment, the influence of the home and of the current structure of social institutions and standards, both handed down from the past, and environment *stricto sensu* — climate, diet available, etc. Educational opportunities may be a mixture of both. The quality of education must depend in part on how many generations have been striving to improve it, but it may also depend on current events.

It is important for the progress of welfare that positions whose holders have influence on the course of events, a wide range of positions, should be manned by those well qualified for the task. This raises problems of jealousy and gives scope for good manners to assuage feelings. In the case of specialised abilities there is less problem, since jealousy is confined to those in the profession; the man in the street does not, if *compos mentis*, repine at not being in a famous orchestra. But where the abilities required are of a more general character — as in politics, business, etc. — there is a double problem (*a*) of the possibility of assessing the extent to which any individual is endowed with the required capacities, and (*b*) the injured feeling of those who remain throughout their lives on the lower rungs, whether they have the required capacities or not.

There may be something to be said for the economic free market system, with all its faults, on the ground that success in it is determined partly by ability and partly by good luck. Failures may console themselves with the thought that they have had bad luck. One might call this the built-in good manners of an institution. I recall a man in a very small way of business in Oxford who had in his youth been the next-door neighbour of the great Lord Nuffield. He liked to narrate the chapter of unhappy accidents, but for which he was quite convinced that he would have achieved a fortune and fame comparable to that of Lord Nuffield. He seemed composed and entirely free from bitterness as he told his tale.

Some might argue that it was a grave defect in the free market system that promotion is chancy, since this must to some extent impede progress. A frightful word, 'meritocracy', was coined some years ago, perhaps the most frightful word within my knowledge. Unlike aristocracy, with its old-world charm, it has the implication that the best qualified deserve (merit) high rank. We like, on the contrary, to think that, because these dreary people are well qualified for their tasks, we have to tolerate their being in high places, *little* though they deserve on wider grounds to be there.

One trouble about meritocracy is that it defeats the wit of man to devise a system that gets the right men into the right places. I doubt if they have a more effective system for that purpose in Socialist economies, in spite of the optimism of Bernard Shaw. The other trouble is that meritocracy, if it could be achieved, would be terribly rude to the unsuccessful. I suggest that it is worth sacrificing a little of material progress for the sake of having a good-mannered society.

I promised earlier in this discourse to say something about death duties. I regret a high level of death duties for two reasons

1. The 'love thy neighbour' form of words introduces an emotional content, as so much required, in order to get compliance with it. By and large, with exceptions of course, fathers (and mothers) love their children. This love gives them a motive to work harder than they would otherwise do in order to benefit them. It is to be noted that hard work benefits the economy, usually, by a greater amount than could be swept into the bag by the said hard workers to benefit their children, even if there were *no* death duties. But very high duties may diminish, almost to vanishing-point, the benefit that harder work can convey to children. Thus they reduce to an important extent the amount of benefit that the rest of society receives *net* by the potential hard work of parents, as motivated by the desire to benefit their children.

2. If I am right in the stress that I lay on genes, it is important that the children of parents (or of more remote ancestors) with efficient genes — as evidenced by the amount

of money that, apart from death duties, they have been in a position to leave their children – should have some initial advantages. By examination systems we can detect potentially helpful and efficient members of the rising generation. As one who has worked through his lifetime as an examiner, in many different kinds of examination, I may be permitted to express doubt as to the 100 per cent efficiency of the examination system in selecting the most capable people in all cases. Of course it has its part to play; it is very good as far as it goes, but it does not go the whole way. It is extremely important that there should be, if possible, a supplementary method for selecting people for the higher positions in our society. I submit that the presence of good genes as evidenced by the money accumulated by parents or more remote ancestors should be a supplementary criterion.

It may be objected that in our capitalist society money may have been earned by parents, etc., by fiddles in the capital market or the formation of conglomerates. It suffices for my argument that a non-negligible proportion of the money should have been earned by hard work that made a real contribution to society. Going back to more remote times, the Crown gave estates to those who had contributed to the efficiency of government. It may be that some grants were made to loathsome time-servers. Again it suffices for my argument that a substantial part of the grants were made to persons who really had done good service.

High death duties blot out much of the evidence supplied by the past about which individuals now living among us are likely to be able to help us most in relation to the increasingly difficult problems confronting us and thereby to increase total happiness.

The fact of inequality must make one raise a question about democracy – 'one man, one vote'. It has the merit of politeness. Winston Churchill is reported to have said that experience of the working of democracy would incline one to think that it must be the worst possible form of government, until one had knowledge of other forms, which were all worse still. In this, I suggest, he did less than justice to the constitutional monarchy of this country in earlier times, a form of mixed government, which ruled the country through its period of greatest achievement and progress. Currently, if someone raises doubt about democracy being the perfect form of government, a frequent reply is, 'Oh, you are a fascist, are you?' As though the only alternatives were democracy and fascism. This suggests a terribly low level of thinking in the present age. But I suppose that there have been comparable idiocies in past times also.

However, I think that on the whole democracy is the best form of government for those peoples with the necessary qualifications. I recall the title of a book by E. M. Forster: *Two Cheers for Democracy*. There is a contradiction in the thinking of some who deplore the advent of elections on the ground that the government is more inclined to dole out popular measures at that time. Is not this what democracy is for? May not the popular measures be better for welfare than rigid adherence to a credit squeeze likely to be based on some dogmatisms of a bureaucracy rather than on valid economic thought? Rousseau favoured democracy because he thought that its system gave people what they wanted to have. But he made the proviso that democracy is acceptable only if there are no political parties. This does not appear to be practicable. What would meet him would be a sort of plebiscitic democracy. Would it not be a good thing for us to have a plebiscite on really important matters, like joining the Common Market or having summer time in winter?

There might be something to be said for a piece-by-piece softening of the abstract rigours of democracy even here. No one resented university representation. Its abolition was actuated by party interests. John Stuart Mill, that great radical, favoured an examination test. In his hands it would have been rather severe, as he knew Greek when quite a small boy.

The advocacy of world-wide democracy seems ill-judged, still more ostracising certain countries which do not conform to it. It does not in fact seem viable in most countries today. It is probable that a build-up over generations, in which certain habits and traditions are established, is needful, as in our case. The Americans in the eighteenth century already had the benefit of our lengthy experience.

Races are also unequal in the sense defined owing to genetic differences. 'Oh, so you are a racist.' 'Oh, so you are a fascist.' All this nonsense!

I hasten to add, lest I be thought guilty of Anglo-Saxon self-praise, that, to the best of my knowledge of various races, I would put the Japanese at the top. And I add also that, in my limited experience, I have not been in contact with any race in whom I have not found endearing and lovable qualities that fully entitle their members to 'equal consideration' and made me feel that they are my 'brothers'.

Of course the Japanese are of mixed race, like the members of most nations. Has any sociologist done a systematic, computer-assisted, investigation of a nation of mixed racial origins to determine which of its characteristics are due to the races present in it in various proportions (the genetic determinant) and which to social and economic arrangements, as historically developed, in the country (the hereditary environment determinant)? That would be exceedingly interesting.

I come to my climax — bad manners one degree removed. A widely proclaimed slogan may, if false, require contradiction in due course, if acceptance of it as true would have a seriously damaging effect on the progress of human welfare. This act of contradiction might involve grave rudeness. The blame for that should lie on the promoters of the ill-considered slogan.

3 Contribution of Economics

TRADITIONALLY, economics has adopted a somewhat normative attitude, especially here since Adam Smith, and in due course in the United States. Its recommendations are based on the principles of utilitarianism, although that word, invented by Bentham, was not known to Adam Smith.

Economics does not cover the whole sphere of pleasures and pains, but only that of 'economic' goods and services. These used to be defined as those capable of being exchanged. This definition is a little too narrow, since one might have a centrally planned Socialist system that found itself able to dispense with exchange altogether; and yet there would still be economic goods. A wider definition would be to say that economics is concerned only with the goods and services of which the constituent items can be made alternatively available to one or other of different persons. Thus goods like friendship or mystical experiences are excluded. Behind the goods, and in some ways more important than they, are the productive resources, which can be alternatively allocated to producing one kind of good or another according to need.

As we have already seen, the mere assertion of the utilitarian principle does not by itself provide specific rules of conduct. From where does economics get its rules?

It has a second maxim up its sleeve. This relates to the use of a free market system. If people have access to a market or to markets, they will choose to acquire those things that give them the greatest pleasure. The free market tends towards the realisation of the goal of utilitarianism.

But there is not, of course, a free-for-all. Prices have to be paid for the goods. The ultimate aim of Communism is that goods shall be unpriced and that people shall be able to take as much of everything as they want. There would be no scarcity. The producers would keep the pipelines full all the time. This seems to be something very remote and unattainable. People's wants are often said to be insatiable. Yet such a state of affairs may not be as remote as it seems. With the rapid advance of technology, it is possible that economic goods could be produced in such abundance that people could have as much (or, maybe, almost as much) as they require. Their 'insatiable' desires would be addressed mainly to non-economic objectives, cultivation of the arts, etc. There might be a few surviving special types of economic goods still not available in unlimited quantities; but these might be a matter of minor importance in relation to the whole pattern of human life. Economics would then fade out as an important subject of study.

Betwixt and between the still remote ideal of Communism and the free market system, we have to consider alternative systems, in which, although goods are not available in unlimited quantities, the market system is not fully utilised, and the allocation of productive resources among alternative uses is largely planned at the centre. It has been common in the 'free' world to refer to centrally planned economies, like that of Russia, as 'Communist'; this is really a misuse of language; countries adopting a centrally planned system should be called 'Socialist', and that is what the countries concerned call themselves. In such systems the market is not entirely dispensed with. People have some measure of freedom about how to spend their incomes, although the variety of choice has been so far rather restricted in those countries. But the allocation of productive resources to alternative possible uses, which in free market economics is largely determined by market forces, is there centrally planned. The bureaucrats are supposed to know what people want, or ought to have. In recent times there has been some tendency in the Socialist countries to pay more attention to markets as indicators of what people want and to adapt their production plans accordingly. The transition is proceeding rather slowly. I was in the Institute of Mathematical Economics in Moscow not long ago. They explained how they were trying to forecast how people would want to spend the extra incomes that would come to them through rising productivity, by field inquiries, which they also carried on, so they said, but presumably in slight degree, in capitalist countries. Their method was to compare the articles consumed by those of a given income bracket, call it X, with the articles consumed by those in the income bracket next above it, and to assume that those now in bracket X would in fact be in the one above it, next year or the year after, or as the case might be; they would want to consume those things which those already in the upper bracket were now consuming. This seems to assume a deadly uniformity of human nature. But if one takes the overall average of a very large group, it may not be far from the truth. Particular individuals would be free to concentrate freakishly on goods particularly to their taste, at the expense of other goods. I feel that even in capitalist societies, there is a rather dreary degree of uniformity when one comes to considering the average of large numbers. The Mathematical Institute worked backwards from the prospective consumption patterns thus ascertained, to the consequent requirements for materials, intermediate products, etc., and informed Gosplan of their findings. By this method the central bureaucrats would be able to have cognisance of the wants of individuals and shape their plans for the future accordingly. How far the bureaucrats take account of the findings of the Mathematical Institute is naturally beyond my knowledge. But I think that there is no doubt that there is a trend in that direction.

I have already remarked that, short of the remote ideal of Communism, people have to pay prices in the market in order to obtain what they want. These prices are themselves supposed to be governed, to a large extent, by market forces. This brings us to what may be thought of as the *pons asinorum* of economics, which has indeed been the central doctrine of traditional economics; but I doubt if all who get university degrees in economics would be able to formulate it with precision.

The prices referred to should reflect costs of production. The pleasure that an individual derives from an article should be measured against the displeasure entailed for those who have to work to make it. Different kinds of productive resources are usually required to work together in the production of an article and, to assess its cost of production, have to be totted up. But for this purpose they have to be valued by some common measuring-rod, like money. One cannot add a day of unskilled labour to a ton of coal beneath the ground. It is by market forces that these various contributors to production, 'factors of production' as they are called, are supposed to be valued. The value of each factor is determined by the value of what it is able to produce, more strictly by the value of its 'marginal' product, but I do not need to go into that.

The immediate reaction of the plain man is to interrupt, 'But surely you are arguing in a circle'. The price (value) of each product depends on the values of the factors of production needed for its production, and the values of the factors of production depend on the value of what they produce. This is the *pons asinorum*. Actually there is no circle. A solution is found by bringing together a large number of simultaneous functional equations, which set out how much pleasure people are capable of deriving from each of varying quantities of all of the different commodities and the powers of the various factors of producing the various products. These equations can usually be solved uniquely, and they specify how much of each commodity will be produced and what its price will be. The whole process of price formation and of the determination of how much of each article is to be produced is settled by market forces and nothing is left to the judgement of bureaucrats. This anyhow is the economist's ideal; there may, however, be sundry deviations from it. I ought also to mention further equations simultaneous with those just referred to specifying the different methods of production of each article ('production functions'). These also can be solved when the whole array is set out.

In principle the Socialist economies also hold that prices should depend on cost. It is asserted that for many years price formation has been very arbitrary in Russia; but this is a manifestation of inefficiency, rather than a neglect of the ideal relation of price to cost in principle. Marx himself, while starting off with simple human labour as the ultimate cost of everything, allowed that superior kinds of labour should be valued at a premium. The fundamental difference between Socialism and capitalism, supposing Socialism to be purged of all its inefficiencies, is not in the matter of price formation; the Socialist aim is to have the price of each article equal to the factor cost, plus a mark-up to provide for fresh capital formation and government expenditure. The fundamental difference is that under Socialism profit in our sense is not allowed; the only way of earning income is to be an employee.

The classical economists were inclined to think that their recommendation of the free play of market forces covered the whole ground. They were willing to grant exceptions where the market allowed monopoly power positions to be built up. Work done in the early thirties of this century, in which I participated, suggested that monopoly was much more all-pervasive than had previously been supposed We referred to 'imperfect competition' or 'monopolistic competition'. After many years of reflection, I am now inclined to think that we somewhat exaggerated the importance of monopoly in producing deviations from what would happen under a fully competitive system and in producing a maldistribution of incomes I have stated my revised views in a *Festschrift* in honour of E. H. Chamberlin, one of the pioneers of the analysis of 'monopolistic competition' in the thirties.

None the less, I hold that the old classical doctrine of the free market does not cover the whole ground, and will be found, as time proceeds, to cover less and less of the ground. We shall come to require more assistance from the sociologists. I have instanced in another context the siting of the proposed new London Airport. By the free market doctrine the choice of the site should depend exclusively on the value of the land required on the one hand and the technical costs of operating the airport in one or another of the alternative sites on the other hand. If, as is normal, the land is privately owned, there would be legal safeguards against the landlords asking a monopoly price. This does not appear to me to be anything like the end of the story. What about other aspects of the site – the nature of the countryside that will be destroyed, of village life previously proceeding, of the social pattern, of educational facilities, of the pain caused to many people by the uprooting? These matters do not find their place in the two values that, according to the market economy view, should determine the choice of site. There is also the question of noise. My guess is that a floating airport in the Thames Estuary would justify tens, even hundreds, of millions of pounds of extra cost. To determine this matter correctly, what has come to be called a 'costs and benefits' analysis is needed. At this point the economist has to turn to the sociologist and should be prepared to become heavily indebted to him. But can the sociologist deliver the goods?

It may be objected that I have chosen a rather special case. But a wider doubt has recently come to be felt about the desirability of the sovranty of market forces. A notable challenge has been made by the distinguished American economist, Professor Kenneth Galbraith. Referring to the United States, he has argued that too much stress is laid on goods and services that go through the market, and that too large a proportion of the total national effort is devoted to producing them. Many goods and services can only be purveyed on the initiative of the government, or of some non-profit-making agency, and it may often be impossible to make those who enjoy the resulting benefits pay a price in proportion to their enjoyment. The taxpayer may have to pay the cost, although the degree to which he participates in the benefits may not be in proportion to the amount of tax he pays. In the United States stress has been laid on the question of the pollution of air and water, and on the *dégringolade* of the centres of large cities. Cars have enabled those of the middle income group, and even many of those in the upper part of the lower income group, to live in agreeable suburbs, while the upkeep of the houses in which they formerly resided has been neglected, and the way of life has become sordid. Cp. p. 2. In fine, slums have been created, in which social standards have declined. Central sites may in due course become wanted for other purposes. What is to be done with their inhabitants? They may have to go for miles to find another slum, far away from the district where they have been habituated to doing useful work. One solution is to erect skyscrapers (known in America as high-rise buildings). This may afford a very bad way of life, especially for children. There comes into my mind memories of the little stone cottages in Huddersfield with their lovely little rose gardens, where people lived a decent life with incomes far below any obtaining in this country at present. Though these questions may not present themselves with a similar degree of urgency in this country, yet we have similar problems, and as time goes on, they will increase. If we look ahead, I am confident that the kind of advice given by Professor Galbraith will apply to us also. The problems involved are intricate and interdependent, and I do not think that the slogan of leaving them to be solved by market forces will get us the right answer. Once again we have a case where economic and sociological studies should merge.

The sum total of economic welfare in a country and its increase are taken to be measured in our statistics by what is known as the Gross National Product (G.N.P.), more strictly by the Net National Product. More and more attention is coming to be given to the course of the G.N.P. by politicians, and indeed by the man in the street. International comparisons are made. The problem of adding up different kinds of goods and services arises; I need not deal with this statistical matter, except for a few points. Public services, not sold in the market, are valued at their cost. By comparison with goods and services conveyed by private enterprise, the public services are undervalued, because in the case of private-enterprise goods and services there is also a profit. And then what about legal restrictions, for example for the preservation of the countryside, or villages or urban centres? By impeding private enterprise in doing what pays best, the restrictions may cause the ensuing G.N.P. to be less than it would otherwise have been, while on the other side no positive gain is shown in the statistics from the preservation of the amenities which in the absence of the restrictions would have been lost. In fine, the restrictions may add to the sum total of human welfare in the years that follow, but by our method of calculation they seem to reduce it. Admittedly the net gain is extremely difficult to measure. Once again one has to appeal to the sociologists.

What about leisure? An increase in leisure is part of the increase in human welfare. A figure for this could be included in the measurement of the G.N.P. Of course it would be needful to draw a distinction between involuntary leisure, unemployment and lack of opportunities to work overtime in the case of those who wish to do so on the one hand, and a shorter working day as negotiated by trade union leaders, etc., on the other. Even here there may be some difficulties. It has been said that in certain cases a shorter standard working day is negotiated, not because the workers desire to work any less than before, but because they want to be paid for a greater proportion of their work at overtime rates of pay. Doubtless there would be many intricacies in such measurements.

I am violently opposed to multiple shift work, except in cases where it is manifestly necessary, as in the maintenance of certain services during the night. People say, 'Oh, but by two- or three-shift systems it is possible greatly to reduce the cost of production by reducing the amount of equipment per man required and in other savings of overheads. 'Do you not realise,' they argue, 'that we have to keep competitive with foreign producers, that we have to keep our balance of payments straight, etc., etc.?' I regard these arguments as entirely specious. We expect our G.N.P. to continue to rise somewhat; in fact we are getting richer all the time. In the midst of this it appears to be quite monstrous to take a retrograde step, such as the introduction of multiple shift working where it has not obtained before.

I favour keeping heavy lorries off the road. 'Oh, but this would increase the costs of transport and make us less competitive.' I am not sure whether a true assessment of the alternative costs of road and rail transport has been done even on orthodox lines. But here again we need a 'cost and benefits' analysis. We have to sum up the cost in terms of fatigue, nervous wear and tear and time wasted by the passenger motorist. He has no means of expressing through the market mechanism the detriment to him due to the presence of heavy lorries on the roads. Of course there is the Parliamentary system. This has seemed to be a very inefficient method for getting people what they really want. However, at the moment I am discussing the market mechanism and its inability to deal with this kind of problem.

I referred to the understatement of the value of some public services. There is the further point that the valuation does not include an allowance for what used to be called 'consumer's surplus'. But this omission applies to the market economy also in a way that I shall describe. Classical economic theory was by its premises essentially atomistic. By this I mean that there was an implicit assumption in the evaluation of any project that it was of small size in relation to the economy as a whole. That being so, one could legitimately have a *ceteris paribus* assumption. One particular project would be too small to affect the value of a unit of labour in the whole economy and too small also even to affect the value of the product that it was designed to produce. This assumption may have been near enough to the truth in most cases in the days of Adam Smith. It may be true of many small enterprises now. But the area of its validity has shrunk since his day.

This comes up in an important way in relation to the less developed countries. There is a widespread opinion, which I personally believe to be fallacious, that in those countries, where capital is short and labour abundant, such capital as there is should be directed into labour-intensive projects, the more capital-intensive projects being avoided. This sounds plausible, but I do not believe it to be correct. Such capital as there is should be directed to those projects which will do most to raise the output of the country in question, per unit of capital employed, whether they are capital-intensive or not. Infrastructure is an obvious case where the project is likely to be capital-intensive and yet highly rewarding in a less developed country.

I said that those projects should be chosen which do most to raise the output of the area per unit of capital used. Can this be abbreviated by saying that capital should be directed to the most profitable projects? I think not. This is where the atomistic assumption of classical economics may lead us astray. Where the project is not very small in relation to the economy as a whole, the extra output resulting from a project is shown, not only in the profit of the enterprise, but also in the excess of the wages paid by its promoters to the workers over what they would have got had the project not been undertaken. This process is very visible in less developed countries, where the existence of an important project causes a certain number of workers to be drawn away from subsistence agriculture where their product and standard of living are very low, and transferred to an occupation where their productivity is substantially higher as evidenced by the wages that they are paid. To get a correct evaluation of the increase of output due to a project of substantial size, both the wages of labour (and rewards of other factors employed) and the prices of the products should be reckoned at their *pre-project* values. Only in this way can we calculate the net addition to the national product caused by the project in question.

What is known as the analysis of static equilibrium, as set forth in authors such as Alfred Marshall, Walras and Pareto, is very elegant and fine-spun. But it is rather tenuous. There is not much body to it. In my young days Alfred Marshall loomed very large. He was thought to have rounded off the general principles of economics, leaving little for the epigonoi to do, except work out their application in specific cases and make descriptive studies of particular parts of the economy. The Cambridge economists were apt to comment on any further venture into ultimate principles with the proposition 'It's all in Marshall'. And indeed, it very often proved to be. But 'all' does not necessarily amount to much. I recall that, when I was talking to Keynes in Cambridge in the twenties, Marshall's *Principles of Economics* came into the conversation. 'Have you not yet discovered,' said Keynes, 'that that is an empty book?'

The general theory of economics has in the past been so slight that I have been led to wonder how great a part it can play in education. I always favoured Modern Greats here, because economic theory was complemented by other mental disciplines. Of course when one moves over to descriptive economics and to statistics, the landscape is vast. Its educative quality is another question.

There is one branch of economics which has a rich content and is still developing, namely national income statistics, including the country's external balance of payments accounts. I would go so far as to say that this is a very good subject for teaching in schools. It calls for precision in thinking, is fairly rich in content, and, being still unfinished, it gives scope for the pupil to think for himself. An illustration of its unfinished character is the present condition of United States balance of payments statistics. Mr Bernstein's committee made a classic report on this subject in 1965. The result of the year's working is now stated in two ways, 'the liquidity balance' which embodies the old traditional way, and the 'official settlements balance', embodying roughly Mr Bernstein's way. These two balances give widely different results, and frequently move in opposite directions. This matter has been further complicated recently by the enlarged importance of the Euro-dollar market. We have American residents lending into it but, recently, far more borrowing from it. It appears to be more difficult to estimate the amount of the former process than that of the latter, for statistical presentation. 'Errors and omissions' are always an interesting and often large item. It has big swings and these suggest systematic causes.

When I hear of economics being taught in schools, I

should like to think that this was a main part of the subject-
matter of instruction. But I have an uncomfortable feeling
that the instructors may be purveying the 'laws of supply
and demand'. What are these? By the law of demand, a rise
in the demand for an article may cause an increase in its
price in certain circumstances, or a decrease in others, or
leave its price unaffected. That is very informative. The
relevant circumstances cannot always be stated in detail with
precision. I believe that the so-called laws of supply and
demand will play only a minor part in the economics of the
future.

I should proceed to Keynes' contribution. Classical economics was very good on the distribution of productive
resources among varied uses and on the equilibrium prices
of particular goods (the *pons asinorum* already referred to).
It was not so good on what got, or failed to get, the economy
to work at its optimum level. There was a general presumption that market prices would secure the maintenance of full
employment, subject to frictions. This was the sphere of
Keynes' major contribution. He held that equilibrium might
be reached with a good deal of unemployment still prevailing. He examined from various points of view the factors
governing the level of aggregate demand, as distinct from
the levels of the particular demands for the various commodities. He was the father of what has come to be called
macro-statics.

I recall that some time in the thirties it was my duty to
write a report on certain projects of our Institute of Statistics
with a view to getting support from the Rockefeller Founda-
tion. I described various projects in the field of macro-
economics and others in the field of micro-economics. My
chairman, an Oxford figure of distinction and renown, still
alive, but not I believe here among us at this lecture, said
that, unless I deleted those barbarous words, he would not
sign the report.

Macro-statics has for a number of years loomed large, but its importance will, I feel sure, prove to have been only temporary. Its elaboration should be thought of as a bridge, but an absolutely necessary bridge, to the development of economic dynamics. I think that I may claim that since 1933 I have recognised that quite different tools would be needed for the development of economic dynamics from those required for micro-statics and macro-statics.

I confess that I am not altogether happy with the progress that has been made since. There has been a proliferation of researches on various relations, especially those that can be computerised, and all this is very valuable. But some of it seems to be going ahead without appreciation of the need in this field for what might be called a geometry, or, if you like, a set of basic axioms. I may have spoken with too much disparagement of Marshall's system, as applied to micro-statics. We still have not developed a comparable set of basic axioms in economic dynamics, and I fear that we suffer from the lack of them.

Some have thought of dynamics as constituting a sort of appendix that can be tacked on to a treatise on statics. That was what John Stuart Mill thought in relation to the early classical economics of which he gave what for long remained the most polished statement. His *Principles* was still a textbook in Oxford when I first came here. Mill thereby killed the dynamic aspirations of the early classical school. Adam Smith and Ricardo were both full of dynamics, although, of course, their propositions are not all acceptable now. The death of dynamics was assisted by further developments of the early classical economics by Karl Menger and Stanley Jevons (both in 1871), who enlarged the scope of the marginal principle, which itself stems from Ricardo, thereby perfecting the early classical scheme of thought. But this perfection distracted attention from the problems of dynamics. I have the feeling that the marginal principle, elegant though it is, is not destined to play so great a part in the development of economic theory as it has recently been playing. I say this, although I may claim to have made a contribution to marginalism in the form of the 'marginal revenue' concept. I am now inclined to think that it has been over-used; I have already touched on this.

My own views on dynamics, which only constitute a first tentative effort in the subject, have been grossly misrepresented by most commentators S. Niconi has made an admirable catalogue of some of the misrepresentations in *L'Industria*, published Milano, 1967 ('On Harrod's Model and Instability'). The persistent misrepresentations have surprised me, since in the case of other expositions by me I have not usually had the reputation for obscurity. I believe that the misrepresentations have been due to a very powerful resistance of the human brain to any new idea. It has a strong tendency to reinterpret and redress the new idea in the light of established doctrines to which it is accustomed; by doing so it will almost certainly falsify the new idea.

I will give one brief example. It is often said that my formulations have rested on the assumption that a constant fraction of income is saved. Incidentally I have always tried to avoid making assumptions, whenever possible. In the formulations referred to there was no assumption; I provided a geometry-type axiom: with increasing output due to neutral inventions, steady equilibrium growth (which may be regarded as a constant velocity) is conjugated with a constant fraction of income being saved (by persons, companies, governments, etc.). But if the fraction of income saved is rising, then the equilibrium growth rate is accelerating. This is not an 'assumption' but an axiom. A constant saving ratio is conjugated with a constant growth rate and a rising saving ratio with an accelerating growth rate. One of the most frequent errors in this field is getting a dimension wrong, e.g. associating the velocity of X with the velocity of Y where it ought to be associated with the acceleration of Y. I am striving in the book on which I am working to deal with these matters in a style less liable to misunderstanding.

It may be appropriate that in this lecture I should say a few words about our present confused state of affairs in relation to economic policy-making. I am sure that our time horizon in this matter is much too short. People have their eyes glued to the monthly trade returns and hold that policy should and must depend on how they turn out in the next few months. It is the same in the United States, where there is a greater stress on the inflation now proceeding there. The Federal Reserve System is expected to make its policy depend on how things develop over a few months. In relation to the objectives and expected effectiveness of measures of public policy, the time horizon should be at least five, or, preferably, ten years. Deviations from the smooth course of progress are to be expected; note will be taken of deviations that seem in relation to previous projections to be supernormal, but only with a view to modifying in due course and after prolonged consideration the ten-year policy targets. Of course there are certain matters to which there should be a rapid reaction, but such reactions should be designed for short-run and relatively superficial effects. Policies determining something so fundamental as the level of employment should not be affected by events that occur in the course of a year.

In both countries, especially in the United States, monetary and fiscal policies have been designed to check price inflation. These policies are of proved effectiveness in reducing (or increasing) the general level of activity in an economy. I am doubtful about their effectiveness in influencing the course of prices, except when the aggregate demand for goods and services is in excess of what the economy can supply. This has not been the condition in the United States (or here) during the last year. In the United States, as each month went by during 1969 and into 1970 without the deflationary policies having any discernible effect on the upward course of wages and prices, the authorities have taken the line 'Have patience; wait and see', as though there were some economic law by which the deflationary measures were *bound* to cause an abatement in the upward movement of wages and prices. There is no such law. There is no fundamental axiom in economic dynamics which states this cause–effect relation. All depends on the particular circumstances of the case, which must be subject to empirical investigation.

As to inflation, which is objectionable for various reasons, it may be that a direct approach to the matter will be needed. This could take the form in the first instance of 'guidelines', moral suasion and education and, finally, if they fail, certain legal sanctions. I use the words 'moral suasion': a moral question is involved here, in accordance with the definition supplied in my last lecture. A sectional wage increase might do no harm, and its promoters might plead that in its favour; but if all other unions in *similar circumstances* secure the same increase, very great harm could be done on the inflation front. This is a case where a moral issue on Kantian lines is clearly involved.

In the United States the Americans had fair success with a policy of 'guideposts' under the regime of President Kennedy and for two years afterwards. Thereafter these were abandoned, although the Democratic Administration was still in power. The reason was this. After a number of years of very fair success with the guideposts in checking inflation, there was a year in which it increased somewhat. It was felt that labour would feel that it should be allowed to catch up on, or partly catch up on, this price inflation, and it was considered that it would be unrealistic to leave the guidepost unchanged at a 3.4 per cent per annum wage increase. On the other hand it was felt that it would seem defeatist to alter the guidepost upwards in order to allow in wage bargains for the price increase that had already occurred. So it was thought better to say nothing either way and abandon the guidepost policy; but this may have been a pity. Under the Republican Administration there has been some ideological change, and a guidepost policy is out of favour, not simply because it is difficult to administer, but as something undesirable in itself. Recently the guidepost policy has been frequently referred to as a 'jawbone' policy; this unseemly word is used to pour a little ridicule on a moral suasion policy. The idea is that these grave matters should not be governed by mere talk, and that a successful fight against inflation may be achieved by the more impersonal method of pressing buttons and pulling levers—money supply policy, Federal budget surplus, etc. But it may be that there is no method of eradicating inflation by pressing buttons.

Furthermore, I suggest that the general preference for guiding the course of events by pressing buttons, as against guiding it by moral suasion, may rest on a misjudgement about how civilisation and economic welfare have in fact progressed during recorded time. Of course there have been powerful forces determining the course of human develop-ment other than *either* moral suasion *or* the pressing of buttons by legally constituted authorities. But moral suasion may have been more important than pressing buttons.

It should be part of sociology to define the potential areas of moral law, and thereby the appropriate areas for moral suasion, not by reference to the feelings or fleeting opinions of the majority of people, but by reference to hard facts. A moral rule is applicable in this case, because, as a matter of hard fact, it belongs to the class of cases where if n people (say unions) act in a certain way, the ill effect will be much more than n times as great as the ill effect would be if one union only acted in that way. If they can establish such cases, the sociologists should commend moral suasion as a suitable policy instrument. After all moral suasion has had effective results on various occasions in the past, and has indeed been quite crucial in certain phases of human history. I confess that I regard suasion by do-gooders to be more altruistic as rather impudent. There is all the difference in the world between this and the use of suasion in the hope that thereby one may gain acceptance for there being a moral law to do or not to do a certain kind of thing. Suasion may turn a potential moral law into an actual one. I hope that I made the distinction between general altrusim and compliance with a moral law plain in my second lecture.

Happily there have been some faint signs of a revival in favour of jawbone in the United States. For instance, Professor Kenneth Galbraith, whom I mentioned earlier, has added a section in the new edition of his *Affluent Society* which comes out strongly in favour of it. Mr George Meany, head of the nearest United States equivalent of our Trades Union Congress, may be mentioned in this connection. Mr Arthur Burns, President of the Federal Reserve Board, and a renowned economist, strongly favours it. Mr Bob Roosa, formerly Under-Secretary of the United States Treasury and inventor of the Roosa Bonds, which have played a big part in the international monetary system, has, although surrounding his statement with heavy qualifications, and recommended a six-month wage freeze.

The levers have in both countries been used from time to time in a way deliberately designed to increase unemployment, even if only by a moderate amount. I strongly object to this. A 1 per cent increase of unemployment here, which is considered trivial, affects in a most distressing way some half a million human beings, including dependants. In the United States it affects about two million. Here the objective is mainly to bring our books into balance on our foreign account. This certainly should be done, but there are other ways of doing it. In the United States stopping price inflation is more stressed. Putting two million people into distress in order to avoid the need for jawbone seems altogether out of proportion. And then there is the background doubt whether the press-button policy will be effective in checking price inflation.

I think that the issue in this case is one of straight altruism. I doubt if a moral issue is involved. Thou shalt not give great pain to many people, in order to avoid taking more complex steps that could achieve the same (desirable) result without giving pain, or nearly so much pain. This holds whether the other fellow (say, some other country) does it or not, and thus strictly belongs to the general code of altrusim and not to the specific one of moral obligation.

Beneath all this fumbling and pathetic confusion, the real fault lies at a deeper level, namely in the unsatisfactory condition of economic dynamics itself. Until we economists can get that subject into better order, so that it can yield clearer and more valid maxims of policy, we must not blame the policy-makers too much.

It may be interesting to observe that, since I wrote what I have just been reading, indeed during the last week, two very important authorities, namely Mr Arthur Burns, head of the Federal Reserve System, with whom I had a long talk on the subject when I was recently in America, and Dr McCracken, chief of the Council of Economic Advisers to the President, who had both at the outset, especially the latter, set their faces against jawbone, have both, according to our newspapers, softened their attitudes in this respect. Mr Burns has indeed come out strongly in favour. I have an uncomfortable feeling that it is not so much the rising unemployment as the large slump in Wall Street that has put on pressure in the United States for a reconsideration of existing policies.

It must not be inferred from what I have said in favour of jawboning that I am fully convinced that we can overcome price inflation, either here or in America, without the use of legal powers, that is direct controls over wage movements. Such direct controls by the public authority would of course be something entirely different from the press-button policy. We should begin, however, by giving jawbone a much better trial than it has yet had.

International monetary policy is in a state of great confusion. In a recent lecture in another place (St Andrews University) I raised the question of what is the sovran power in this field and listed five possible contestants for this honour, if it can be so called. These were the international Monetary Fund, the Group of Ten, the gnomes of Zürich, the informal group of central banks that organises swap credits on an *ad hoc* basis, and the Federal Reserve System of the United States of America. To this there ought probably to be added the Gold Pool countries, sometimes known as the Group of Seven, for the limited period from the autumn of 1960 to March 1968.

I will not endeavour here to specify their rival claims to sovranty. The International Monetary Fund is, of course, the recognised authority. It has done, and continues to do, much good work. It is probably its presence that has saved us from severe currency disorders of the kind that prevailed for most of the time between the two world wars. It administers the system by which countries can get temporary credits from it, to tide over periods of deficit. It enters into regular consultations with its member countries, and these may sometimes have been of value, especially to less developed countries, such as those of Latin America. It may impose conditions when its facilities are used. Again sometimes, but not always, these may be salutary. In its outlook it embodies conventional wisdom to a large extent, but is probably more liberal than a representative central banker.

The 'Group of Ten' is not a self-appointed group of

important countries, as I believe many readers of the financial columns of newspapers suppose. It was officially established by the International Monetary Fund, on the initiative of its Managing Director, Per Jacobsson, in 1961, in connection with the General Arrangements to Borrow, a scheme whereby the solvency of the International Monetary Fund, in recurrent danger owing to its defective structure, was underpinned. I would suppose that the Group of Ten has a stronger claim to being in effect the sovran body than the International Monetary Fund itself. It is to be noted that when at long last in 1963 it was recognised by the conservative conventional wisdom of the central bankers that there might at some future date be some shortage in the medium for international settlements – in fact there had long since been one – it was to the Group of Ten, and not to the International Monetary Fund itself, that this question was referred. In the Group there was severe internal conflict. It took four years to reach agreement, and this was only achieved within a month of the meeting of the International Monetary Fund at Rio de Janeiro in 1967, when the plan for Special Drawing Rights was approved. Tribute should be paid to the vigorous chairmanship of Mr Callaghan. Even then it took another two years to get agreement about the date of activation of the plan. The S.D.R. scheme came into operation on 1 January of this year.

During the discussions it was seriously put forward that we should have a sort of formal bicameral constitution for important decisions about international money, the International Monetary Fund and the Group of Ten – or some body of similar constitution – *both* having to agree on any important change. Although this idea was not adopted, we may be sure that *in practice* prior agreement by the Group of Ten will be required before any substantial change is made, including a continuance of the S.D.R. scheme after its initial three years.

The gnomes of Zürich are wrongly named. 'Gnomes' suggests mischievousness, whereas the people in question are honest and well-intentioned people doing a difficult job. They are the foreign exchange advisers to multi-national corporations and other companies that have international dealings of significant amount. The layman is led by a loose use of language to suppose that, when there is a 'run' on a currency, this is mainly due to speculation; on the contrary, much the greater part of a 'run' is usually due to precautionary covering and hedging, when the advisers believe that there is some chance of a change, upwards or downwards, in the official par value of a currency. These advisers are spread around the world and do not live in Zürich. That city is indeed an important centre of international exchange operations; its experts are on the telephone to London every morning, where our experts give their views. I have thought in connection with the runs on sterling, which were so tiresome for us between 1964 and 1969, that 'gnomes of London' would be a more appropriate expression. I suppose that this telephoning is one of the reasons why we have to endure this tiresome summer time in winter.

These gnomes began to be important only after the restoration of the convertibility of the important currencies in 1958. They have been responsible for the changes of the par values of currencies since then; the movements of funds advised by them when they considered that a par value might (or ought to be) changed, have been at times so great as to force the hands of the authorities; it was only by a ruse that the French gave the appearance of devaluing the franc in 1969 when not under pressure.

If the gnomes in effect determine when changes in the par values of currencies are to occur, have they not a good claim to be considered sovran?

The informal system of swap credits organised by the central banks is intended to be an offset to the operations of the gnomes. When the gnomes advise a movement of funds that is in the aggregate massive, the central bank of the currency under suspicion is provided with credits to meet this movement. Thus these informal arrangements, which lie quite outside the ambit of the International Monetary Fund, may be deemed to constitute those engaging in them as a sort of counter-sovran. But they have not always succeeded in their objectives.

It is to be noted that these credits are supposed to be used only to offset runs and not to finance deficits in the basic balances of external payments of countries, for which resort must be had to the International Monetary Fund on a temporary basis. Thus there is an implicit, but fairly clearly defined, division of labour between the two sovrans, the International Monetary Fund and the informal group of central banks extending mutual swap credits.

I believe that I am right in saying that the total amount of resources made potentially available by the informal stand-by swaps is greater than the amount of resources available through the International Monetary Fund.

Finally, the distinguished American economist, Professor Kindleberger — and there are others who think on his lines — says — I am not quoting him verbatim — 'Why all this fuss? The U.S. dollar is in fact used as the world money. One must not judge things by formal constitutions, but by what actually happens.' If this were correct, it would mean that The Federal Reserve System of the United States was the International monetary sovran. This viewpoint, however, is not internationally accepted.

And although in many respects strongly pro-American, I have certain qualms. The Federal Reserve has succeeded in the last sixteen months in causing a recession in the United States followed by a Stock Exchange collapse without succeeding in terminating price inflation there. Is the whole world to become involved in this unhappy outcome?

Furthermore I believe that, owing to the vagaries in this same period of the Euro-dollar market, the intricacies of which it is too late for me to start describing to you, there is likely to be a severe dollar crisis in the period ahead, which will damage its world-wide image.

Before leaving international money, I ought to refer to yet another body – Working Party No. 3 of the Economic Committee of the Organisation for Economic Co-operation and Development. It has been assigned the task of determining, and has published a report on, what countries ought to *do* when they are in balance of payments difficulties. What is the proper 'adjustment' process, as it is called? Its report was well considered, but did not claim to have solved the 'adjustment' problem. This brings us back to the deeper question of the continuing unsatisfactory condition of fundamental economic theory and doctrine.

I have referred, I feel in too personal a manner, to my disquiet about the state of dynamic (growth) economics. I hoped more than thirty years ago that my fundamental equations of great simplicity – I believe that in mathematics simplicity is reckoned a virtue – would inspire economists to develop a wider system of dynamic axioms, as distinct from the static axioms that we already have, but this has not happened to any great extent.

I have referred to 'costs and benefits' analysis. This takes us outside the field in which economic precepts flow naturally from giving priority to the unimpeded workings of a market economy as constituting the supreme precept. This is where sociology is needed. I shall not today deal with the present position of sociology. Waiving that, for cost and benefit analysis it is essential that sociologists have some acquaintance with economics, but if there is at present no adequate economics for them to understand, that is a problem. Highly refined static economic theory may in many cases be of little use. In some respects it could even give wrong pointers, e.g. in emphasising the importance of movements along a static production function.

There is, or should be, as part of dynamic analysis, the idea of an optimum. This is not too difficult in relation to an insulated economy. But that is different from a typical modern national economy. Part of the quest for an optimum, which includes the optimum rate of interest and optimum minimum acceptable return on capital, involves the optimum capital flow between countries. This should not be estimated without reference to the interests of trade or investment partners. And so, to determine the optimum for one country we must have reference to the optimum of other countries. One has in mind here especially the optimum of the less developed countries.

To be quite frank I do not think that it will be possible to determine the optimum for ourselves or anyone else without some kind of a world plan. That is a formidable prospect! The plan would have to be based on what is called an input–output analysis for each country and an estimate of elasticities of demand, which affect the 'foreign exchange bottleneck', which is so particularly important for many of the less developed countries. We require a world plan, which need, however, only be based on rough estimates. Is it altogether unfeasible, considering the vast number of researchers around the world, some of them competent, devoted to economics? But we also need the basic growth axioms, and that is where we are particularly lacking. I am afraid that the main culprit for the lack of sufficient organisation on behalf of less developed countries is economics itself. There are also, of course, political obstructions. To devote sufficient national resources to a world plan and to modify domestic policies in accordance with it is just what the political powers in each particular nation are as yet unwilling to agree to.

4 Is There a Social Science?

During my time at Oxford I was subject to surveillance, so far as my duties to the University were concerned, by the Social Studies Board. That seemed a dignified name for it, and I was happy to be in connection with it. As regards my college duties, my lifelong title has been Student of Christ Church. I was always well content with the dignity of this appellation, although aware that in its historic origin it marked inferiority. None the less I preferred the title to that of Fellow. The latter, I believe, has the connotation – we shall be hearing more of connotation today – of having a share of responsibility in the management of the corporate endowments of the college. By worldly standards this may be grand, making one a man of property. I preferred the more academic title, which indicated how in fact I have spent my life, namely in study.

I have to confess that I lapsed from grace for a brief period a year ago, wishing at that time to be regarded as a scientist. When I lost my rooms in Christ Church, I had erected in my garden in London a prefabricated hut to house my very voluminous library of series of reports containing statistical information. The hut is an object of limited life, and I accordingly thought that I was entitled to a depreciation allowance on its cost for income-tax purposes. I made an appeal to the local Commissioners of Income Tax on this subject, one of whom has been graciously attending these lectures.

In order to get my allowance, I had to establish two

points, namely (1) that I was a trader, and (2) that economic research was 'scientific' research. I took the first point first, since, if I did not get over this hurdle, it was useless to proceed further. I claimed that I was indeed a 'trader', since I peddled my wares to newspapers and other periodicals in many countries, thereby earning this country valuable foreign exchange. It was in relation to this that I erected the hut. Had I been content to be a 'gentleman' economist, I could have found room for my library of volumes, or for those worth preserving, in my house. When writing such articles as I do about current events, I almost always base them on a survey of past trends, maybe over a five-year period, or a ten-year period, or the period since the war, or even going back before the war. It is for this purpose that the very voluminous files are needed.

The Commissioners held that I was certainly not a trader. To be a trader, one had to peddle material goods; services did not count. It is rather curious that the British law should still be making this distinction between 'productive' and 'unproductive' labour, reminiscent of the eighteenth century. Russia is still old-fashioned in this way. That is the present state of British law.

I was also told emphatically by H.M. Inspector that the law does not recognise economic research as 'scientific' research. In regard to this, I was proposing, should I have won my round as regards 'trader', to call in aid the Royal Economic Society; Sir Alexander Cairncross offered me his good services. The upshot is, that, as the matter stands, like it or not, British law does not recognise economics as a science. Perhaps I should have said British income-tax law; that is perhaps the most important part of British law; anyhow it is the one that gives most employment to people.

You may think it unworthy that I should have briefly striven to get myself recognised as a scientist for the sake of a beggarly thousand pounds.

Historically the word 'science' has been applied only to a part of the wide area of systematic investigation. One associates this word particularly with the laboratory experiment, although this may not be a necessary feature in all cases. I may go back to the trinity, which I rejected as having anything to do with the explanation of valid induction, but which is characteristic of some sciences – hypothesis; elaboration, if necessary, of its consequences by deductive processes, in which other well-established premises must also come into play; and verification, whether, as usually, in a laboratory or by field exploration. The hypothesis usually expresses a functional relation, and, if the hypothesis is fully verified, it becomes a law. In most advanced sciences this law is not a mere formula with adjustable parameters; definite numbers are supplied for the parameters. This may be a rather exacting requirement in some cases; but most sciences, I think, would claim that they have a reasonable expectation of reaching this status.

So far sociology, to use a less provocative word than social science, has not yet reached this stage, indeed is very far from any reasonable prospect of reaching it. I would make an exception for demography, which might reasonably be a candidate for scientific status. Sociology is altogether lacking in what I have called laws and not very rich in precisely formulated hypotheses. Even its definitions are apt to be somewhat amorphous. I would strongly stress that this rather primitive condition makes its study *more* difficult, and not the other way round. I do not refer to the creative efforts of a Newton or a Clark-Maxwell. For the ordinary working scientist there are guideposts as to what next needs doing and good prospects of being able to advance his subject. Even negative results from a well-conceived set of experiments may be valuable. In sociology, it is to be feared, there are often not even negative results. There are no results. 'No' in this context is not the same as 'negative'.

A sociologist must be in greater doubt which way to proceed. It is more difficult to select hypotheses likely to be worth testing. And the methods of testing are ramshackle. All this makes the studies covered by this generic word more difficult than those of the well-established sciences.

Why then is there this mad keenness to have it called a science? Is it because this word is more prestigious with the man in the street, with the ignoramus, let us call him, in consequence of its nuclear bombs, space travel, etc.?

I fear that this nomenclature, if accepted, could do harm, by giving younger workers wrong ideas, e.g. that to get good results, one should strive to imitate the procedures of the natural sciences. Get out a project, establish a questionnaire and an area of field investigation, collect a mass of figures and put them into a computer. Result: usually nil. What is not enough appreciated is that in these immature subjects the ratio of sheer hard thinking to project activity should be much higher than in the more advanced disciplines. I have referred to the current trend to downgrade thinking already. It can do especial harm in sociology. This is one reason for doubting the wisdom of its laying claim to be a 'science'. 'Political science', a much older expression, was perhaps also a mistake. I may refer again to Modern Greats, where it has been called more simply and appropriately 'politics'.

I was sitting next to Keynes in the autumn of 1922 at the High Table of King's College, Cambridge. He was just back from Berlin. There he had been summoned, along with the Swedish economist, Gustav Cassel, and two other economists, whose identities I now forget, to advise the German authorities about the appalling difficulties they were having with the German mark, the value of which was rapidly sliding down towards zero. When the news was released that these four men had been summoned to Berlin to give advice, the mark had a spectacular rise in the foreign exchange market. Unhappily it was only temporary.

Despite the state of the mark, they had a festive dinner in Berlin, and Keynes was placed next to Max Planck, of Planck's Constant and founder of the quantum theory. Planck informed Keynes that, when young, he had had the idea of becoming an economist. But he soon gave it up, because he found economics too 'difficult' for him. What he had in mind, of course, was the lack of clear guideposts, to which I have already referred, about what should be done to advance this study. Lowes Dickinson, a very charming and distinguished person, whom perhaps one should call a sociologist, was sitting on the opposite side of the High Table and piped up; 'That is a funny thing', he said. 'Bertrand Russell once told me that, when he was a young man, he had thoughts of becoming an economist, but gave them up because that subject seemed too "easy".'

I fear that Bertrand Russell comes the worse out of that story. Incidentally, to revert to manners, was not Lowes Dickinson's remark rather rude to Keynes? Perhaps at a High Table all is forgiven; one can look forward to the port. I certainly had for many years a colleague at Christ Church High Table whose rudeness was unflagging and, perhaps, unequalled. The point is that, if Bertrand Russell had devoted his whole life to economics, he could not have achieved anything of comparable value to the achievement of Keynes, because he lacked Keynes' intense realism and deep-laid common sense. These qualities are more necessary in the social studies than in mathematical logic.

Having told this slightly unfavourable story I must hasten to pay my tribute to Bertrand Russell, great Englishman and great eccentric. We all deeply grieve his recent death, even at the age of ninety-seven. I did not know him well, but my relations with him were happy.

I have already mentioned during my discussion on inductive logic the work of Jean Nicod. At a certain point I wrote to Russell to ask if he knew anything about the French originals of Nicod's two works. He at once produced them for me. I made a translation of some pages of the *Geometry* which I sent him. He summoned me to tea and we had some talk about the desirability of a new translation. He then rose from the tea table and went over to his desk, where he wrote out a check for one hundred pounds, as his contribution towards publishing costs. He was not a rich man. It was done so simply and charmingly and without any fuss.

There is thus an extra personal touch in the grief that I share with you. Had he lived only a few months longer, he would have seen the new edition of Nicod, and that would undoubtedly have given him great pleasure.

To revert to the question of why sociologists are not proud that their subject should be called a branch of 'study', with its implication that this is more difficult than one of the regular sciences, this may spring from a desire to draw a line between themselves and certain other studies. I quote from Mr George Homans, 'What makes a science are its ends, not its results . . . all the social sciences qualify – even history. The humanities do not. Much fiction, for instance, is very true to life, but the standard by which fiction is judged is certainly not in general this kind of truthfulness.'

This is surely very superficial. Fiction does not state general propositions, although in a writer like Tolstoi it may come near to doing so. Some branches of creative literature are entirely irrelevant in relation to building up knowledge in depth about human nature. But not all. Some novelists have shown a very profound knowledge of human nature and an understanding of social relations. They have not proceeded by formalised projects or questionnaires, but by direct observation. In some areas that may be the best, and even only, way of reaching important truths. Novelists are especially interested in the emotions, which play such a prime part in social relations. Sometimes they even stand on the brink of mystery itself; anyhow they understand something of the intertwining between man's sense of mystery and his emotions. Sociologists cannot afford to ignore all the vast mass of material that is gathered together in the great literature of the past. Without disrespect to the sociologists, I would say that the novelists of a certain type have already brought together a much deeper and wider range of knowledge about social relations than is ever likely to be obtained by project research. The point is that these writers had supernormal powers of understanding certain things in depth which are very rarely given to the general run of men. I would think that in any compulsory sociology reading list for students – I use this word in the American, not the Christ Church, sense; it is convenient because it dispenses with the need to specify whether one means undergraduates, graduates, or both – some great novels, like *Moll Flanders*, *Middlemarch* and *The Return of the Native*, should always be included. And poets, too, have their contribution.

'Bright star, would I were steadfast as thou art.'

Sociologists may object that they know all about that, but that they are setting about their task in a different kind of way. Is this division of labour really viable? Does it make sense? It may certainly lead to a great waste of time. A questionnaire is prepared. A man who knows about human nature by direct observation may say, 'I can tell you the answer – it is plainly yes (or plainly no). The people questioned probably will not understand what the question means and lead you to a false inference.' Or what is asked may be a nonsense question.

Most of what we know about human nature and social relations and their development through time is embedded in our great literature. It is really too foolish to think that all that can be neglected.

It is bold of me to address you on this subject, since I am not a professional sociologist. From time to time during the course of the years I have read some of the classics of sociology – de Tocqueville, Max Weber, Durkheim, even Mannheim, and with a little dip into Talcott Parsons. In preparation for this lecture I have been reading some of the up-to-the minute treatises. Of the earlier sociologists the one who made much the deepest impression on my mind was Henry Maine. Towards the end of my time at school my Classics had got a bit rusty – I later refurbished them to read Greats – and I went in for the New College History Scholarship. Maine's *Ancient Law* was a set book for that. Having read it, I read all his other works with avidity, about such topics, as I dimly recall, as land tenure in early Ireland.

Lord Longford had a story that he thought to be very damaging to Stanley Baldwin, whose faults are writ large in our minds. He was taking a country walk with the Prime Minister, who recalled his college days. 'The book', he said, 'that made the greatest impression on my mind in undergraduate days was Maine's *Ancient Law*, with its concept of the development of society from status to contract.' And then a troubled look came over Baldwin's face. 'Or was it' he added, 'from contract to status?' Frank's scorn was unlimited. This was the book, of all books, that had made the greatest impression on Baldwin's mind, and he could not even remember, as regards one of its central themes, which way the stream flowed. I think that Frank was a little hard on Baldwin. He should have been given credit for recognising the magisterial quality of a concept by which the confused events of social history could be given a pattern. Baldwin's various avocations in his post-undergraduate days did not make it needful for him to retain in his memory which way the stream flowed.

In contemporary sociology there appears to be a very high proportion of methodological discussion. Is this appropriate for a subject that is admittedly in a very early phase?

One would think that the proper time for the methodological analysis was after substantial successes had been
achieved in the main corpus of the subject. At that
point one might say, 'Let us take a self-critical retrospect.
What have been our methods? Have they been logically
valid?'

Definitions appear to play a very large part. I will trouble
you with only a few examples, taken from *Sociology* by
Leonard Broom and Philip Selznick, a favoured textbook.
'Societies may be called familistic when the family is the
main type of dominant group.' Or again, 'Acculturation
refers to a group's taking on elements from the culture of
another group.' Acculturation! What a ghastly word! I have
found it in other works on sociology. These sociologists are
supposed to be experts on culture. In fact they often put
culture in the forefront of what they claim to be researching
into. Most of their recent writings are replete with linguistic barbarisms, clear evidence to my mind that the authors
themselves are quite uncultured. Otherwise they could not
bring themselves to use the words they do. Can uncultured
people make effective inquiries into the inner being and
nature of culture? They do recognise, to be fair to them, the
great importance of language in the social set-up. It is a
vehicle, not only of communication but of culture. I think
that it would be difficult for a student to do a course in
modern sociology and be submitted to a sustained barrage
of linguistic barbarisms, without coming out of it a somewhat less cultured person than he was before he took the
course. And if a large mass of citizens are rendered less
cultured by taking these courses, the average level of culture
in our society will decline. I am genuinely nervous about
this. By contrast the language of books on the natural
sciences is usually quite satisfactory. Terms are defined with
precision and explanations go forward in a workmanlike
manner. There may be too many mathematical symbols for

the taste, or abilities, of some of us. But that is required by the subject-matter. I have used the word 'cultured'. My form-master at Westminster School, John Sargeaunt, abhorred this as a barbarism. He held that we should say 'cultivated'.

Another definition: 'The process of building group values into the individual is called socialisation.' This usage I have found in a number of works on sociology. Do the sociologists not know that the meaning of this word is pre-empted in important works of history and famous treatises and also in common parlance? It is used for a process that is first cousin to that denoted by nationalisation. Do the sociologists live in such a remote ivory tower that they do not know this? Ivory is something rather beautiful. I sought for a word of less pleasing denotation to express the same thing. Or do they think themselves so important that they can ride roughshod over a widespread usage and displace it? They cannot. It is time to pass on to constructive propositions.

In 1938 I was President of Section F of the British Association for the Advancement of Science. This was the Economic Section. At that time sociology had no footing in the British Association. I am not sure how the matter stands at present. In our committee I suggested that it might be a good idea to give the sociologists an afternoon during our week's session. We agreed at that time that Morris Ginsberg would be the most suitable person to read a paper. Accordingly I wrote very carefully to him. I explained apologetically that I did not want to leave him quite free to choose his subject, although that might seem rather an unorthodox procedure. The economists had agreed together on a particular subject that would be of a special interest to them and appropriate to the occasion. Would he take any one constructive proposition in sociology deemed to be true and explain to us the kind of evidence on which it rested? I suggested that the discussion provoked would be

SMM D 2

quite sufficient to occupy the meeting. He wrote to me agreeing to my proposal. He came and read his paper. There was much discussion in it of various notable authors and the scope of their studies. But no constructive proposition was mentioned.

I expostulated with him afterwards. I reminded him that he had promised to supply us with one single proposition in sociology and discuss the evidence for it. He replied, 'Oh, well, you know, sociology does not go in for specific propositions'. This was a perfectly clear statement, and not necessarily derogatory; and I bore it in mind.

I may be forgiven for referring again to Mr George Homans. In his little book *On the Nature of Social Science* he is at pains to stress that sociology does contain constructive propositions. Emphasis is given to a proposition quoted from Berelson and Steiner, 'When a response is followed by a reward (or "reinforcement"), the frequency or probability of its recurrences increases'. Homans adds, 'This I quote as a proposition about the effect of the *success* of a person's actions on its recurrence' (p. 36).

Two pages later he gives a more elaborate formulation: 'The main proposition of the rational theory in one of its forms may be stated as follows . . . in choosing between alternative courses of action, a person will choose the one for which, as perceived by him, the mathematical value of p multiplied by v is the greater, where p is the probability that the action is successful in getting a given reward and v is the value to the person of that reward.' This does not seem to be a tremendously world-shaking proposition, entitling it to the pride of place that Homans gives it. Two things about it struck my mind.

1. There is the absence of any statement to the effect that if 'success' occurs on two or three or more occasions, the probability that similar action will have success rises more than in proportion to the number of occasions and con-

sequently the likelihood that the agent will take similar action again. There is no hint of any knowledge about the process of inductive inference. Yet it is precisely at the primitive level at which sociology now is that simple induction might be thought likely to play a greater role than it can in the more mature sciences. Do sociologists know about the principles of induction?

2. The word 'value' is unashamedly thrown in. The author does not seem to appreciate that this is a red-hot word. You cannot just let it drop without explanation or definition, especially in a work purporting to be very careful, methodical and even scientific. Perhaps the author has dealt with this matter in other writings. Even so there should have been a reference to his standpoint in the text where he sets out his fundamental proposition. I have always avoided the use of the word 'value' to the greatest possible extent. In economics it is quite all right, since there it stands for something precisely defined, value in exchange. In the old days it was sometimes used also for value in use, but that expression has been superseded by utility.

For most of my active life, or any how for the later part of it, I have been distressed to observe the infiltration into, and later the proliferation within, the corpus of economics, of the expression 'value judgement'. This expression is obnoxious to me and I regard it as a great stifler of thought. I confess that I may have used it on occasion, but usually in verbal debate. You may be arguing with someone, with whose general position you entirely disagree. At a certain point you ask, 'But does not what you say imply a value judgement?' This may produce the complete collapse of the antagonist. This I am afraid may have verged on dishonesty, since I truly have been unable to give a meaning to the expression 'value judgement'.

Perhaps I may be permitted a digression on this expression, although it is not, I think, one much used by sociologists. That is certainly a mark in their favour. But it relates to terrain with which they are, or should be, concerned and its use is very widespread.

Linguistically a value judgement should be a species of judgement. The simple question one has to ask about a value judgement is whether it possesses the property of being either true or false. If it does not possess that property, it is not strictly correct to call it a judgement at all. Some hold that a value judgement should really be regarded as an 'emotive noise'. In that case the suasions in question should be couched in the language of poetry and not in seemingly factual statements. Some hold that it is essentially an expression of the personal subjective preference of the speaker or writer, 'I like so and so'. In that case it is intrusive. We can do without statements of these personal preferences. Or does it aspire higher and claim to express the speaker's assessment of what most people like? In that case it appears to take on the 'true or false' property, and constitutes a challenge to empirical investigation, designed to assess its claim. But this does not seem to be quite what people do mean. There is a 'take it or leave it' nuance about it, which seems incompatible with a large project of investigation regarding its truth.

While in the end there may be success in rolling back its intrusion into economics, there are areas which many people believe that these value judgements can claim as their own. I refer particularly to ethics and aesthetics. If they have a proper area in ethics, that will surely lead on to politics, and so to a wider field of social studies. I believe that these ideas are due to confused thinking, or even to lack of thinking.

In an earlier lecture I defined ethics as the study of all that flowed from a single overriding imperative, 'Thou shalt love thy neighbour as thyself'. One uses some such word as 'ought' for what should be done if the imperative is to be obeyed throughout a vast ramified field. The study of 'ought' becomes strictly empirical, like all other systematic or scientific studies. It is a question of ascertaining whether a specific imperative relating to a specific case does indeed stem from the overriding imperative or not. To find the answer to this it is necessary to have knowledge of a vast interconnected field of social relations, the nature of which in due course we hope that the sociologists will be able to analyse. The important point is that the truth or falsity of the ethical sub-precept, given the overriding imperative, is a matter of hard fact. Mention of the word 'ought' suggests to the minds of some that we are deviating into an area – say the area of these so-called value judgements – in which it ceases to be possible to say whether a proposition is true or false. Lack of recognition of this could debar sociologists from investigating many matters that it is important for them to investigate. It is not legitimate to reply to the proposition, 'You ought to do so and so', by saying, 'I disagree, I have different values'.

The only way in which the truth of a subordinate ethical judgement can be called in question, otherwise than by an analysis of the facts of the case, is by challenging the overriding imperative. That is of course legitimate; but if the challenge were limited in this way, it would greatly reduce the area in which argument, based on merely subjective ideas, could legitimately take place. If an interlocutor challenges the overriding imperative, then one is entitled to ask him what his overriding imperative is. It is impossible to legislate against individuals having private overriding imperatives. But one can at least have a rule that, if they reject the great overriding imperative that has for so long held sway over so wide an area in civilised society, they must state their alternative. Let us have a look at it.

I believe that the futility of this kind of controversy would soon become apparent. If it were thought necessary to make a vast study of social interrelations, based on each different private overriding imperative, we should get into a terrible mess. And, so far as useful propositions were concerned, we should probably get nowhere. It appeals to common sense to accept the overriding imperative that I set out at the beginning of my second lecture and see what follows from it. This procedure would offer sociologists a vast field of investigation, subject to empirical tests. The questions that they would be asked to pronounce on would be factual questions, namely the emotional and pleasure-giving content of all the millions of different kinds of social complexes. This would be in line with the way in which they characteristically like to approach matters. If we view the whole thing in this way, the content of ethics becomes the most important area of sociological study.

I next pass to aesthetics. At this point lovers of value judgements will pipe up and affirm that here at least is a scope for them. I do not agree. I hold that aesthetic judgements, like ethical judgements, are true or false absolutely. But I hasten to add that I do not think that this is an area in which sociologists can hope to make headway.

When I was a boy there was an aphorism much quoted in cultivated circles, 'I do not know anything about painting but I know what I like'. This came to be widely referred to. If you wanted to be especially sarcastic, you would give the words a pronunciation not quite in conformity with the Queen's English. The aphorism was quoted by cultivated people in terms of extreme scorn. I believe that aesthetic judgements are subject to the true–false criterion, but that the method of establishing truth is somewhat different. Aesthetic pleasure is something specific, recognisable by those who enjoy it. It is a specific kind of pleasure to be obtained from the mere contemplation of visual forms and sound sequences. It is also to be observed that some people have a greater susceptibility than others to enjoyment of this specific kind of pleasure and to enjoyment of the various sub-species of it. In the study of the matter special attention should be given to the reactions of people of this type. But the true and false alternative depends not only on the choices made by the more sensitive people at a given point of time. It is necessary to integrate through stretches of time, preferably through centuries. This makes valid judgement in the short term, e.g. about 'modern' art, impossible. We shall never know the answer for certain, but then we never know anything for certain; we may get a high degree of probability after the passage of centuries. I recall that a few years ago I took 'Jop' (Lindsay Millais Jopling), lawyer, then very old, son of Mrs Jopling Rowe, one of the most famous Victorian hostesses of literary people, to see the superb beauties of Christ Church Library, recently redecorated. In the hall we had to pass a bust of Dean Lowe, formerly Dean of Christ Church, by Jacob Epstein, one of our most distinguished sculptors. He paused for a moment and said, 'I suppose that art historians of the future will regard this as the most decadent age of art in human history.' I cordially agreed with him. Of course, I may have been wrong. I should like to make an exception in favour of very recent architecture, which strikes me as superior to anything that we have had for more than a century.

From whom should we hope to get provisional answers now about aesthetic merit? Art experts, who can be identified, do not seem to be always reliable. Nor do practitioners either, although they are perhaps a little more so than the experts. There may be another class of persons, who are more aesthetically sensitive than either the experts or the practitioners, but it is exceedingly difficult to identify them. In the nature of things sociologists cannot be expected to give us any clues.

But at the practical end of their studies, e.g. when planning for urban renewal, they should, by the greatest happiness principle, extending it through time, seek the advice of persons believed to have aesthetic sensibility. Who exactly these are is difficult to ascertain, but an attempt to do so will probably be better than nothing.

I hope that sociology, as it progresses, will effectively limit, and eventually eliminate, the area in which these so-called value judgements are brought into the argument.

Reverting to Homans, I should like to quote a passage that seems to indicate that in sociology there are internecine controversies of an obscure but fierce character. He is quoting a passage from Davis and Moore. First the quotation, and then the comment. The quotation runs: 'Social inequality is thus an unconsciously evolved device by which societies ensure that the most important positions are continuously filled by the most qualified persons.' Although this is a little too simple and not wholly acceptable – I hope that in an earlier lecture I have dealt with this subject with a little more subtlety – yet I should have thought that it had some merit as an approximate opening statement, to be modified later. Homans comments on it, 'This last statement is a good example of the length to which functionalism will lead otherwise intelligent men. As Dante would have said, "Let us not talk about it, but look and pass by".' Why this terrific attack on a seemingly innocuous generalisation? It is doubtless because Davis and Moore figure in the mind of Homans as 'functionalists'. We see here some deep divide of an almost theological character.

I return to my quest for constructive propositions, to ascertain whether the Ginsberg dictum still prevails. There is a fairly recent (1964) ponderous book by Bernard Berelson and Gary Steiner which is often quoted, entitled *Human Behaviour and Inventory of Scientific Findings*. Note the 'scientific'. One object, as I understand, of this book was to meet the criticism that sociology is insufficiently rich in constructive propositions. Its 'findings' may be taken to be such, and there are accounts of how the conclusions were reached. I naturally was not able to cover the wide ground. It occurred to me that I ought to adopt a formal and strict method of procedure, to safeguard myself against the suspicion that I was unduly critical and cavilling in my choice of propositions to be cited. I decided to establish a rule for selection and to adhere to it with absolute rigidity. I have taken the last proposition – the 'findings' are all numbered – on every hundredth page (there are over 600) and the last proposition in the book. I omitted only propositions that were inset in the page and clearly subordinate corollaries. I made the decision in advance of action and did not look ahead to see what my harvest would be, so that I hope that I am giving you a fair sample. I am afraid that the first quotation is the longest.

Bottom of p. 100 (B-3): 'Which stimuli [within the field of perception] get selected [for attention] depends upon three major factors . . . the nature of the stimuli involved; previous experience or learning as it affects the observer's expectation (what he is prepared or 'set' to see); and the motives in play at the time, by which we mean his needs, desires, wishes, interests and so on. In short what the observer wants or needs to see and *not* to see. Each of these factors can act to heighten or decrease the probability of perceiving, and each can act on both exposure and awareness.'

Bottom of p. 200 (B-24): 'Connotations are remarkably similar among similar people.'

Bottom of p. 300 (A-4): 'The more severely a society controls sex training in childhood, the more restricted its own sexual practices are likely to be in adult life.' (Is that true?)

Bottom of p. 400 (B-41): 'The greater and more complicated the technology (a) the greater the bureaucratization of the economy; (*b*) the more the skills needed in the labour force; (*c*) the greater the disparity between the skills needed at the top and the skills needed at the bottom; (*d*) the fewer the resources devoted to the agricultural segment; (*e*) the greater the proportion of the labour force in service occupations as against primary production [the authors do not tell us the proportion in manufacturing production; presumably they do not know]; (*f*) the more productive the system; (*g*) the less important the place of individually owned property and hence the more important the organizational rules; (*h*) the greater the reliance on industrial innovation (i.e. the spiral contained in the "faith in technological progress").'

Bottom of p. 500 (B-1): 'There is a tendency in most human societies for people to prefer their own kind and to stereotype ethnic outgroups, especially lower-status ones, in a regular fashion.'

On p. 595 there is a finding that goes on for six pages. I have taken the opening sentence and the last sub-clause on p. 600.

Bottom of p. 600 (A-9.10): 'The major differentials in human fertility are the following, most of them for modern western nations . . . higher fertility among Catholics than among Protestants, higher among Protestants than among Jews.'

Bottom of p. 655 (last in book): 'Upwardly mobile people and those of higher socio-economic status tend to acculturate faster than their non-mobile counterparts. Even within deprived ethnic groups, the more middle-class members are more acculturated to the larger society than are the lower.'

In the course of my lectures I have referred to sociologists from time to time. I have suggested certain problems which they might devote themselves to solving. Perhaps they have solved some of them already? Or perhaps I was too starry-eyed? However, with the lapse of time, much may change in these studies. May I remind you of some of the problems. I am afraid that my list is miscellaneous and very unsystematic.

1. Sociologists are asked to provide short-cut laws con-

cerning human behaviour avoiding the need for a physical examination of the brain.

2. If the working day is cut by 2 per cent, how much of the time released will be devoted to 'do-gooding'? Actually that is the kind of question that they might be ready to answer, although I would not trust them to discriminate accurately between deployments of time and energy that were altruistic and those that were not. Apart from altruism I cannot see them in their general assessments giving the high priority that I do to contemplating a zen Buddhist lake of gravel.

3. 'It is the task of sociologists to get an even deeper understanding of the interconnections of the parts of our social structure in terms of ways of life, economics, environment and above all of the emotional content of various social relations, being a boss, a middleman, the lowest-paid type of employee in a factory, etc.' To make headway here we need to have great sensitivity to subtleties in human nature, as deep as that of Daniel Defoe, George Eliot or Thomas Hardy. The kind of propositions that I have just been reading to you are of course entirely out of the running.

4. I asked sociologists to investigate the maxim 'Spare the rod and spoil the child', and to consider the possible relation between a growing disregard of this and the current increase of crime and violence.

5. I asked them to consider the vital part played by tradition in relation to Kantian morality. As a factual matter they do investigate the influence of tradition. But I have the feeling that they do not sufficiently stress the vital importance of the nexus between tradition and the maintenance of Kantian morality without which our various societies would crumble.

6. The sociologists were challenged to make a survey in a nation of mixed race to demarcate what are the national characteristics (hereditary environment) and what the racial

characteristics (genes). The Americans would make a very good case study since, apart from small minorities, they have such very marked national characteristics. But the component races have also retained some identity – the German Americans, the Jewish Americans, etc.

I have lived long enough in the United States to learn that their society is much more rigidly stratified by occupation and income bracket than ours. How many American sociologists appreciate this?

7. I have held that sociologists ought to be able to assist in the siting of the new London Airport; and more generally, wherever a cost-benefit analysis involving non-economic items, is required. Urban renewals is another case. They are indeed trying their hand at this.

8. I have appealed to them for the formulation of new methods for calculating the G.N.P., having regard to welfare gains due to restrictions on private enterprise.

9. I have appealed to sociologists to get rid in due course of the expression 'value judgement'. I think that this is in line with their typical approach.

10. 'It should be part of sociology to define the potential areas of moral law, thereby the appropriate areas of moral suasion, not by reference to the feelings or fleeting opinions of the majority of people, but by reference to hard facts. A moral rule is applicable in this case [wage restraint], because, as a matter of hard fact, it belongs to the class of cases where, if n people (say unions) act in a certain way, the ill effect will be much more than n times as great as the ill effect would be if one union only acted in this way. If they can establish such cases the sociologists should commend moral suasion as a suitable policy instrument. After all, moral suasion has had effective results on various occasions in the past, and has indeed been quite crucial in certain phases of history.'

11. I asked sociologists to consider likely effects of the intellectual decline in the general run of religious mentors.

12. To anticipate – I ask them to examine the proposition that it is inevitable that the majority of schoolteachers should be of mental calibre below that of those schoolchildren who should be of greatest concern to us.

I return to an earlier theme. It is my view that the most important data capable of enriching sociological study and research are to be found in the great imaginative literatures of the past, extending through the centuries. It is here that we find the results of thinkers who have had far deeper insights into human nature and social arrangements than most of us can claim. I shudder to think what the result would be if one tried to classify by a scheme of categories the various propositions that are implicit in their imaginative work.

There does seem some intellectual difficulty in formulating the concept of a growth of knowledge (for example, of sociological knowledge) when that knowledge is not formulated in any general propositions. We are apt to think of knowledge as embodied or capable of being embodied in propositions. Yet this does not seem to correspond with the facts of the case. Individual A clearly has a much greater understanding of human nature than individual B. But what propositions has A supplied us with? None. Perhaps, after all, Ginsberg was wise in his generation. Apart from the great works that have the deliberate form of poetry or fiction, there are also classic works of sociology *stricto sensu* that do not embody laws, formulae or hypotheses. I might cite *Lark Rise to Candleford* by Flora Thompson and *Akenfield* by Ronald Blythe.

Sociology requires much information about facts, notably statistical information. There may be a horror story; it is relevant to ask, how *many* people are affected in that sort of way? Winston Churchill, whom I served during the Second World War, had a marvellous understanding of this kind of problem. Did it make sense to provide servicemen, many of whom were, increasingly, just clerks in offices, with twenty times as many pairs of trousers as were allowed on the ration to civilians, who were also contributing substantially to the war effort?

Sociology is, or should be, a subtle blend of factual information and understanding in depth of human nature. To formulate how these two very different kinds of knowledge intermesh should be the task of sociological methodology – I apologize for that appalling mouthful! I have been reading too much sociology lately. One trouble is that those who are good at statistics are usually different in person from those who understand social relations in depth.

Sociologists snobbishly want to be reckoned as scientists. This has led to an effort to establish that they are capable of formulating general propositions of a scientific character. It is my view that the propositions, as instanced in Berelson and Steiner, are not of a scientific character, and that their wish to be reckoned as scientists is misjudged, and may be even an 'escape' from the more difficult problems that confront them. It is misjudged also, because to be a 'scientist' is not more distinguished than to be a 'student'. It is misjudged also because it gives a false indicator of the way in which the young, who may be passionately interested in what can be done in sociology, should direct their minds.

Meanwhile we are surrounded with very pressing problems. There are the Indian villages. Mr Chaudhuri, born and nurtured in East Bengal, a very distinguished author, has affirmed that the writer who has understood Indian human nature best was Rudyard Kipling. How many who go out on Foundation- or consortium-financed missions to that country study him thoughtfully? Perhaps some do.

There are the appallingly difficult problems of urban renewal in the United States that I have already referred to. There is a mixture of races of unequal qualities on average in relation to the more skilled jobs. Interference by the courts of law with certain social practices seem to be rather of a copybook variety and not to take account of the more subtle problems. There are in fact problems of infinite delicacy resulting from *de facto* inequalities in certain respects, certain social habits that the legal judgements cannot easily alter, the claims of brotherly love and of tact and good manners. Here is a challenge for the young sociologists. They may have to forget about the general treatises that they have read at the university; but then later the experience gained by coming face to face with these difficult problems in the field will enable them to write specialist studies, in which the wisdom of the great novelists may still be seen between the lines. My guess is that the time at which we can have general sociological treatises of a worth-while character is still very remote. It is not, I would judge, at present a good educational subject.

It is said that it would be an unwarrantable encroachment on the time available for schooling to teach the children Greek. What are they now taught at school? I confess that I do not know. It is inevitable that the majority of school-teachers should be of mental calibre *below* that of those schoolchildren who should be of greatest concern to us. That is a sociological proposition of very great importance. I have not seen it formulated. Of course, there will always be exceptions. John Sargeaunt at Westminster School, to whom I have already referred, was one of the most cultivated minds, to use his favoured word, whom I have ever met. I recall being disappointed, when I came up to Oxford, at not finding among the dons anyone quite of his calibre. It is to be feared that the number of such men who opt for school-teaching as a profession is diminishing.

School curricula should be so devised as to safeguard the children from the vagaries of teachers. That, I think, was inherent in the traditional subjects – a sphere in which traditional wisdom should be highly respected. Matters of relevance for present problems should be avoided at schools – and very carefully selected at universities – because it is hardly possible to avoid the mere prejudices of instructors being imported; and this will destroy the educational value of what is purveyed.

Arithmetic is more or less proof against the vagaries of teachers. I recall reading in H. G. Wells that he felt frustrated when his teacher insisted, with disciplinary sanctions, that seven times eight made fifty-seven. This must surely be rare. In those days at a simple school there may well have been no school store from which a multiplication table could have been obtained. If my understanding is right, the method of teaching arithmetic at school has been revised, so as to reduce the need for a child to use his brains. This, if so, is a pity. The decimalisation of our coinage will have a by-product which is retrograde in this respect. Sums, like long division, in terms of pounds, shillings and pence, made just the right amount of call on the thinking power of a child of eight or nine. Arithmetic cannot occupy the whole time, and, as you know, some minds of great distinction are allergic to it altogether. And only children of some precocity can advance very far into the realm of higher mathematics when below the age of thirteen. The same probably applies to natural science, apart from the mere memorisation of facts, which should indeed be a part, but only a minor part, of the education below that age.

Of course there are vast masses of facts in geography and history. These have their place; but the training of memory, although essential, should be a subordinate feature in education

The learning of foreign languages has a supreme quality for young children. Differences of syntax call into play logical powers, but not, like higher mathematics, to a degree that may be beyond their capacity. Furthermore, in the case of languages, there is not much scope for the teacher to cloud the issue by his own idiosyncracies. Above all, Greek and Latin may be commended for this purpose. Their syntax is further removed from what is familiar, and the superior intellectual qualities of those languages give excellent training. They do not have equivalents for much modern jargon, so that the child has to analyse the underlying meaning, if any, of that jargon, when he is called upon to translate it into Greek or Latin. I am unhappily not qualified to say whether Japanese would fulfil these purposes equally well.

When I hear of more money being spent on education, I sometimes gloomily wonder whether this ought not to be said to be on diseducation, on fuddling the minds of the next generation. Quite apart from the educational value of the process of learning Greek for those under thirteen, I have the idea that time spent at school on acquiring it would not be wasted if it enabled those reaching universities to read Aristotle in his native language.

The object of education should be to send its victims into outer life with minds furbished with powers of analysis, precision and accuracy, and, above all, objectivity, as needed to assess the data presented to them by the raw materials of life, if they go out into practical activities, or by literary sources or field-work findings, if they opt for sociological study. For neither purpose, at present, is instruction in sociology, at undergraduate or graduate level, even with the best intentions of the instructors, suitable.

Is sociology a science? I hope that I have given you sufficient reasons for thinking that it ought not to be so considered, and, more important, sufficient reasons for thinking that it ought not to *desire* to be so considered. But I hold that, in this phase of human history, it is the most important subject of adult study.